SUCCESS WITH
TABLESAWS

SUCCESS WITH
TABLESAWS

MICHAEL BURTON

GUILD OF MASTER CRAFTSMAN PUBLICATIONS LTD

First published 2006 by
Guild of Master Craftsman Publications Ltd
Castle Place, 166 High Street,
Lewes, East Sussex BN7 1XU

Text © GMC Publications/Michael Burton 2006
© in the work GMC Publications 2006

ISBN-13: 978-1-86108-468-2
ISBN-10: 1-86108-468-4

Production Manager: Hilary MacCallum
Managing Editor: Gerrie Purcell
Project Editor: Stephen Haynes
Chief Photographer: Anthony Bailey
Additional photography as listed on page 170
Managing Art Editor: Gilda Pacitti
Designer: John Hawkins

Set in Palatino and Frutiger

Colour origination by Wyndeham Graphics
Printed and bound by Kyodo Printing (Singapore)

Contents

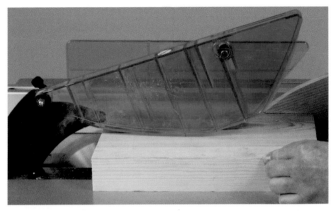

Part 3: Making and Using Jigs

Introduction

I know why there are so many people who love chopping wood. In this activity one immediately sees the results.

Albert Einstein

Acquiring your first tablesaw is quite a major event. For me, it was certainly a step up the ladder, a statement that I was serious about working with wood, that I had made an investment for the future. The commitment was both financial and personal. It was also something that I have never regretted, and I still take great satisfaction in using my tablesaw whenever I can.

As my skills built up over the years and work requirements became more complex, my present machine, a tilt-arbor cabinet saw, purchased along with a workshop I took over, has always been up to the tasks in hand. Though it no longer has youth on its side, with occasional adjustment and routine maintenance it has given me years of reliable service.

This book offers a general overview of the tablesaw and what can be achieved with it. It includes a survey of what is available, a guide to the machine and its maintenance, an outline of health and safety issues, and an account of the most important techniques – including some of the many inexpensive jigs which you can make yourself to improve the speed, accuracy and safety of your work. I wish you the best of luck in your ventures.

SAFETY

All machinery is potentially dangerous, and must be handled with care. Provided you pay attention to the safety advice given in this book, there is no reason why you and your tablesaw should not be perfect workmates in a long and fruitful partnership. All of my digits remain intact and I have no known respiratory problems. The same should apply to you, as long as you treat your machine and your own wellbeing with respect.

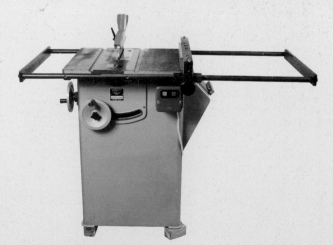

My old faithful cabinet saw.

Part 1:
The Tablesaw

1.1 Introducing the tablesaw

The tablesaw can be defined as a machine for the effective cutting of wood, sheet stock and other materials by the process of passing the workpiece across a saw table and through a motorized circular saw blade. But this basic definition fails to convey the many possibilities achievable when the tablesaw is used to its full potential. This book is intended to guide you towards that goal.

In Part 1 we will look at the machine itself, considering the various types available and how to choose between them. The salient parts of the machine are described in some detail, as is the process of setting up and adjusting them to give the best possible results. Blade selection is important, and we shall look at the different kinds and their particular uses.

Tablesaw types

ABOVE Portable saw.

ABOVE Site saw.

ABOVE Cabinet saw.

This book will concentrate on the three main types of motor-driven saws available for the popular market, all of which come under the umbrella term of 'tablesaw':

- the portable saw
- the site saw
- the cabinet saw.

More specialized types range from the model-maker's saw, designed specifically for craftwork, to the huge computer-controlled machines used in large-scale industrial production. Several alternative terms may be used to describe the same machine, and to avoid confusion the most common of these are listed below.

Some cabinet saws may have a sliding table or carriage fixed to the body cabinet, which moves smoothly along a rail in line with the main saw table. This feature allows for more accurate cutting and easier handling of larger stock, especially sheet material. Americans refer to this type of saw as the **European saw**.

Other machines include the circular saw facility amongst other functions. The **flip-over saw**, for instance, combines a circular saw bench with a **mitre** or **chop saw**, in which the saw blade is raised above the workpiece so that it can be pulled down onto or

---

⊙FOCUS ON:

Tablesaw terminology

Portable saw
also called: circular saw bench, bench-mounted saw

Site saw
also called: contractor's saw, home-shop saw

Cabinet saw
also called: bench saw, panel saw, dimension saw

In this book, when I refer to the **tablesaw**, I mean the cabinet saw unless otherwise stated.

ABOVE A 'European saw' with its sliding carriage set up.

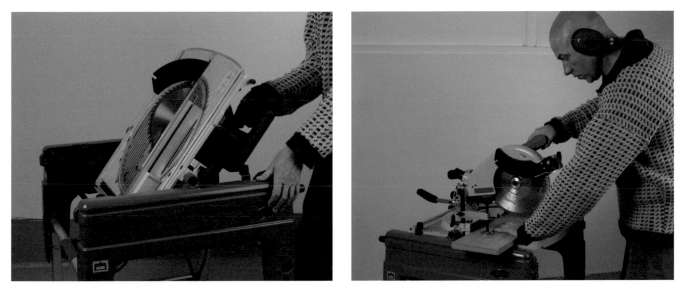

ABOVE and ABOVE RIGHT Flip-over saws are invaluable for site work.

across it for rapid cutting. The blade also arcs to the left or right for angled cuts, and has the facility to tilt up to 45° for compound mitre cuts – all useful functions, especially when working on site.

Combination or **universal machines** include a circular saw table as part of a whole array of options for cutting and shaping wood, such as a planer, spindle moulder and sander, amongst others. Some recent European models are especially well designed, offering considerable potential in limited spaces.

A **pull saw** has the look of a standard circular saw table, but a knob or lever protruding from the front panel allows the blade to be pulled towards and through the workpiece, instead of 'feeding' the work into the blade in the usual way. Increased accuracy is claimed for this type, and in terms of safety the pull saw is certainly an improvement, with little reason to place your hands close to the rotating blade. At present this type of saw can be found predominantly in site work, and is more expensive than traditional site or contractors' saws.

Which tablesaw best suits your needs? To answer this question you must consider your budget, the space available, the kind of tasks you wish to accomplish, and the amount of time you can devote to its use.

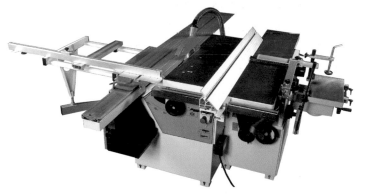

ABOVE A combination machine packs a lot into a small space.

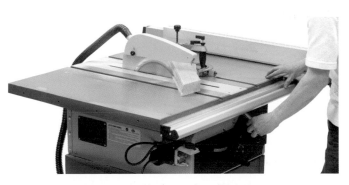

ABOVE Making an angled crosscut or mitre on the pull saw.

The portable saw

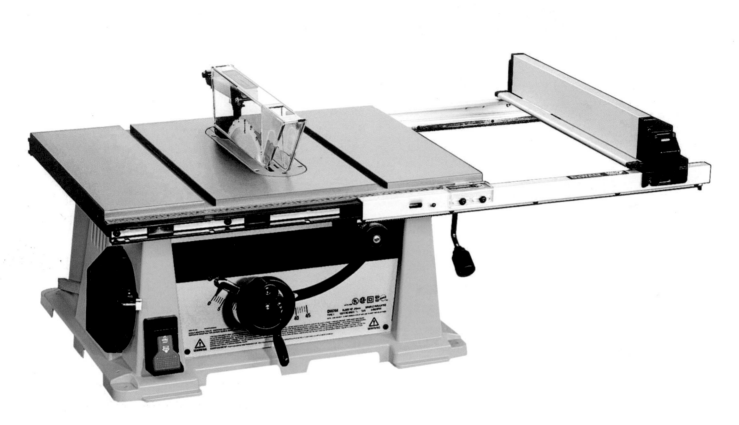

ABOVE A lightweight portable saw.

This is often the first port of call for the hobbyist or first-timer. A growing number of this type of saw can also be seen on site, and, given a solid stand and additional 'outboard' support (see page 32), many larger-scale woodworking jobs can be tackled with confidence.

In recent years both the power rating and the blade capacity have tended to increase – an important consideration, as a larger blade will permit a greater depth of cut. Blade size is typically either 8 or 10in (200 or 250mm), and this measurement is often referred to in the model name. Competition amongst manufacturers has resulted in more accurate fences, less noise and vibration, greater stability and better dust extraction. Most models are supplied without legs, ready to be lugged around single-handedly, but legs can often be bought as part of the package. If not, then a well-constructed home-made stand will suffice – perhaps a small cabinet, which could be mounted on wheels, providing it is fitted with good-quality brakes.

A well-maintained portable saw should operate effectively for years, and because it is relatively inexpensive it can be a wise choice, unless your workload is heavy or you intend to tackle fine furniture-making.

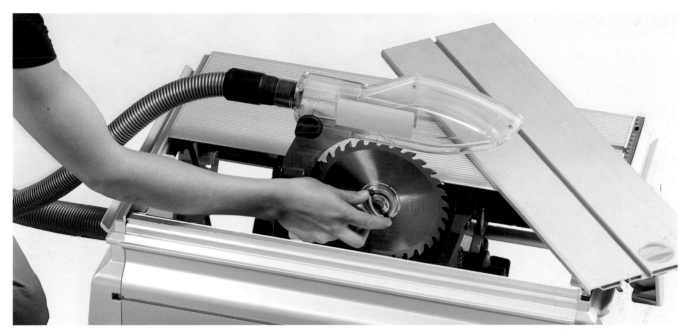

ABOVE Portable pull saws are small but very capable.

ⓕFOCUS ON:

Portable saw pros and cons

For

- Compactness and light weight are invaluable for use in confined spaces, for tidying away after use or for lugging around on site. A typical weight of under 70lb (31.7 kg) is almost exactly the European Union's permitted weight for a work item that one person can carry.

Against

- The portable saw tends to be noisy, and many models are subject to quite heavy vibration because of their lightness. This may mean that parts need to be readjusted for correct alignment on a regular basis, so if your work requires a high degree of accuracy this may not be the best saw for your purposes.
- Because the infeed side of the table – the side on which the workpiece is fed into the saw blade – is small, handling pieces of wood of any great width or length can be tricky; and these saws generally struggle with hardwoods over 1in (25mm) thick.

The portable pull saw

Several firms now make a portable pull saw which combines standard circular sawing with a movable blade that is pulled through the timber. This means safer cutting, as hands are kept well away from the blade; it also allows for cutting grooves or housings (dadoes) on the underside of the timber, where the blade does not pass fully through the wood. This can only be done with the blade guard removed, and this operation is a great deal safer on the pull saw than on a conventional tablesaw, where it is not recommended at all (see page 83). The workpiece should still be clamped in place if possible.

When accompanied by the whole gamut of accessories available, pull saws and other portable saws can be extended into complete saw centres, while still remaining portable.

The site saw

ABOVE A typical site saw.

Not really so different from the portable saw, but more often seen in workshops, this is an altogether tougher, sturdier product, designed for greater accuracy, and capable of a wider range of work with bigger and harder stock.

The tables of these saws are large and solidly built, sometimes from sheet steel, cast iron or a die-cast aluminium alloy. The motors use either 110 or 240 volts, sometimes being dual-voltage. In the UK and Europe, where mains voltage is much higher than in the US, the lower-voltage option is safer for site work, just in case someone should inadvertently sever a cable.

Weighing up to 200lb (90kg), site saws are movable, but two people may be needed. Some models have retractable wheels which do not interfere with the overall stability of the machine. Other variations include the flip-over saw described on pages 12–13.

RIGHT Site saws are only a little less manoeuvrable than the smaller portable saws.

FOCUS ON:

Site saw pros and cons

For

- The powerful motor is often located under the table, giving improved balance, reduced vibration and thus more stability.
- Compared to portable saws, site saws have stronger motors, flatter tables and better dust collection. The fences are sturdier and longer, so cutting sheet material is a more manageable operation, though proper all-round support will always make the job easier and safer.
- You can make or purchase accessories and upgrade certain features. Longer fences and extension tables allow greater accuracy; motorized feed tables, which move the work through the blade at a constant rate with no need for pushing, make for safer operation.

Against

- Some models are on the flimsy side, and these can be inconvenient and time-consuming to use. Go for a high-end model if you can.

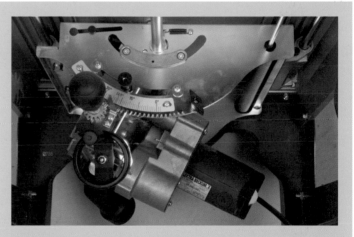

ABOVE Site saw motor fixed to the underside of the table.

ABOVE Additional support enables the site saw to cope with large stock safely.

The cabinet saw

ABOVE A typical cabinet saw.

For more advanced woodworking, where accurate dimensioning is essential and large sections of hardwood are to be worked, you may plump for a more stationary machine in which a floor-standing metal cabinet encases the saw's innards.

It is highly likely that this saw will be the centrepiece of your workshop: every piece of timber will pass through its blade at least once, which means that it will be in use more often than any other piece of equipment, and probably for longer periods of time.

Some site saws have also adopted the cabinet style, but they remain inferior to cabinet saws proper, where the motor and blade assemblies are fixed to the base unit. This means that blade, table and fences will remain more stable and true, and once set up and aligned properly there should be little need to

worry about cuts being inaccurate. With site saws, where the motor is fixed to the underside of the table, there is a greater chance of movement because of direct vibration, so regular checking is needed.

ⓕ FOCUS ON:

Space requirements

Given the standard size for sheet material of 8 x 4ft (2400 x 1200mm), the saw must have around 10ft (3000mm) of clear space in front of, behind and to the left of the blade. To rip up to 4ft (1200mm) in width it should also have 56in (1400mm) to the right of the machine. So, ideally, it should sit in a space measuring 20ft by 12ft 6in (6000 x 3800mm, or 6 x 3.8m).

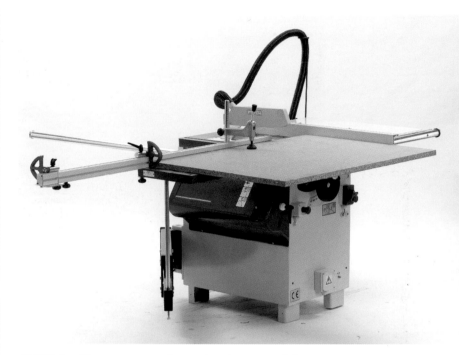

ABOVE A cabinet saw set up for cutting sheet material.

The motors which run these machines are large and powerful, often between 3 and 5hp. But it is the overall weight or mass that singles out the true cabinet saw. Everything about it is heavier: the table, extension wings and some of the internal components are likely to be cast iron. You don't really want to be manoeuvring this machine into its rightful position more than once in its life. Because it is essentially a stationary piece of equipment, space becomes an important factor.

Dust control is crucial, even in a small-scale operation, and the enclosed cabinet on this style of saw helps to contain a good deal of the stuff. Dust collection from both above and below the table is the most effective method, along with an external microfilter if possible. This topic is covered in more detail on pages 98–9.

FOCUS ON:

Cabinet saw pros and cons

For

- It is a stable and durable machine with considerable cutting capacity.
- The components are milled to close tolerances, giving an accurate finish and permitting fine, professional work.
- The enclosed cabinet helps to contain dust, though a proper dust extraction system will still be needed.

Against

- To take full advantage of the saw's capacity you will need to devote a lot of space to it.
- It is substantially more expensive than the portable machines.

Combination machines

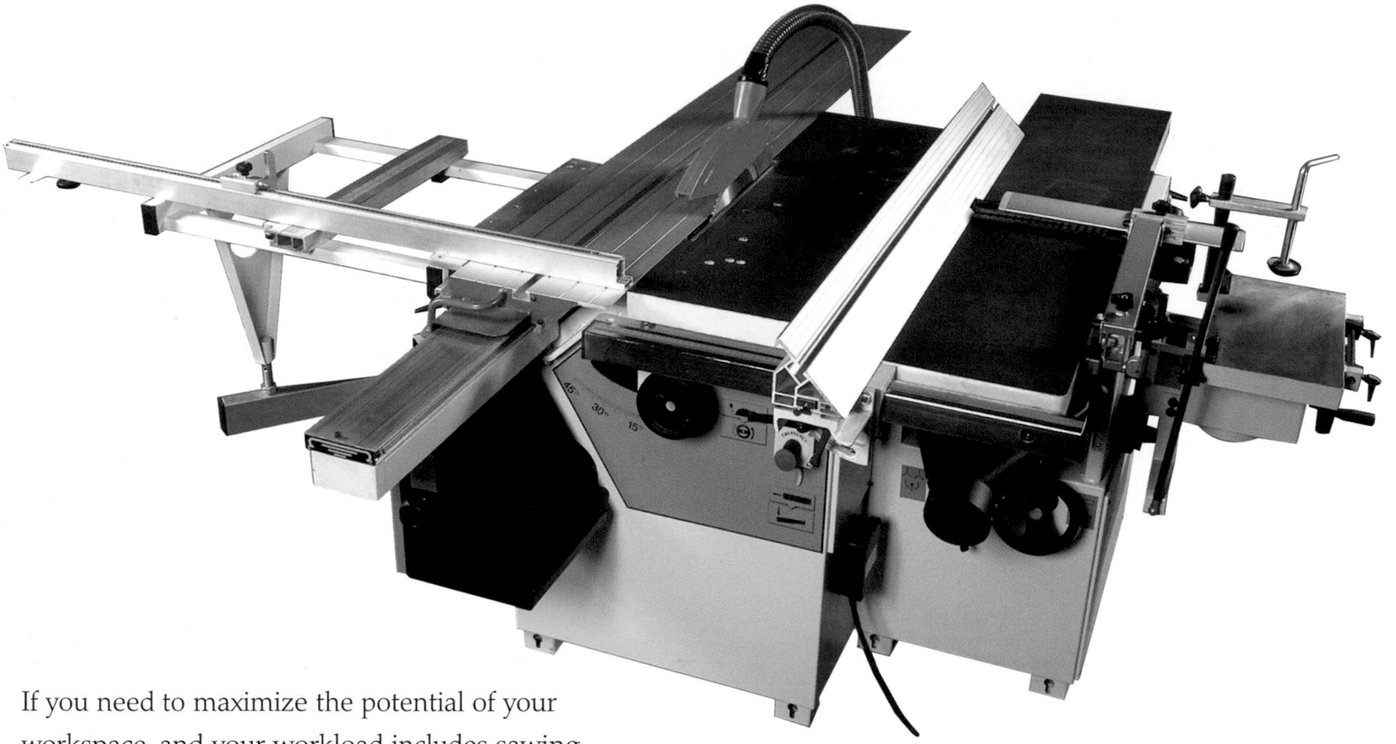

ABOVE **The multi-tasking combination machine.**

If you need to maximize the potential of your workspace, and your workload includes sawing, planing, thicknessing, some mortising and even some spindle moulding, then this type of machine may be the answer – not without a hefty price tag, of course. In recent years these machines have been somewhat scaled down in size, functions and price to accommodate a more domestic market, and wheels have been fitted to aid manoeuvrability – but portability is not one of their strong points.

A strong disadvantage of such machines is that settings may have to be changed on one operation in order to perform a different function, and this can be frustrating. Also, a well-ordered mind is needed so that functions can be carried out in the most effective and efficient way possible in order to minimize the time and energy spent. This, of course, is very good discipline – but having separate machines dedicated to each function gives you more freedom of choice, and is my preferred method.

(**FOCUS ON:**

European and American differences

Traditionally, American saws have made less use of safety devices such as blade guards and riving knives (see pages 34–9), which were felt to get in the way of certain cutting operations. However, this seems to be changing as the more stringent European rules on health and safety are adopted by American users.

With many American and a few European saws, it is possible to mount a dado or shaper head to the arbor, giving a greater range of cutting options; but this facility is not available with the shorter arbors on most European machines. The use of dado heads is strongly discouraged on safety grounds in any case (see page 83).

The sliding table

The sliding table or sliding carriage, invented by Wilhelm Altendorf in 1906, has long been a popular feature in the European market. Running parallel to the stationary main table by means of a supporting rail and runners, it permits more accurate dimensioning and easier, safer handling of large pieces of timber. Not surprisingly, this device is now a growth area in the American market.

Sliding tables themselves can come as accessories or add-ons, but are often supplied as an integral part of the main saw table. The integral sliding table has a superior guide-rail system, making the cutting operation far more effective than using the mitre gauge to crosscut materials. A large, adjustable mitre fence often extends all the way to the blade, helping to support the timber, which is moved through the blade purely by the moving surface of the sliding carriage.

Once you have used the sliding carriage you will not want to go back to the standard table, but, as you may expect, it's the cost that will prevent many woodworkers from taking up this particular option.

With a little ingenuity it is quite possible to design home-made support devices which have some of the same advantages, and with an extended mitre fence good results can be produced without the expense of a sliding table. A bolted or hinged support can be fixed to the main table, and even a corresponding parallel mitre slot cut into it, in order to house runners for an auxiliary mitre fence.

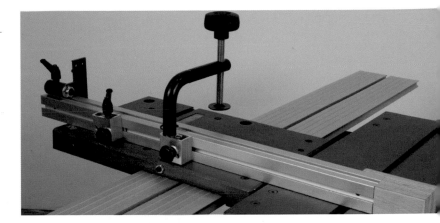

ABOVE **The sliding table permits more accurate cutting.**

ABOVE **Detail of the guide-rail system on a sliding table.**

ABOVE **A sliding carriage with adjustable mitre fence and stop for cutting work to a consistent length.**

Buying used saws

This is an option that is certainly worth considering: there is a buoyant market and some bargains are to be had, but only if you are diligent. So long as you are aware of what to look for and what to avoid – just as when buying a new saw – it is possible to pick up powerful, high-spec saws that might otherwise be out of your price range.

Where to find them

The Internet has provided a dynamic platform for buyers and sellers alike, whether they be individuals looking to sell equipment on auction sites, or companies who deal in second-hand equipment. Simply type 'used tools' and the name of your town or district into a search engine, and off you go. It is simple enough to get technical specifications from any number of woodworking machinery sites, and there will often be a review section giving the low-down on particular makes and models. Some

websites have online woodworkers' discussion groups and chatrooms, where information and ideas can be exchanged.

Woodworking magazines also carry reviews, possibly in more depth. In many areas there is a magazine selling used goods – often with an associated website – where woodworking tools and machinery are usually well represented. Failing that, the classified section of your local newspaper should serve.

Many equipment dealers do good business in used or reconditioned machinery, and some offer trade-ins. There is often a good stock to choose from, and if you are lucky there may even be a warranty.

I have had little success with auctions. Everyone wants a bargain, so bidding will always be high, but it's fun to do and you may have more luck than I have.

ABOVE A second-hand saw in good working order can give excellent value for money...

ABOVE ...though you might have difficulty obtaining spares for the model shown here.

What to look for

Now it can be a tricky business buying used goods, and if there is a no-return policy attached you may be buying into a whole heap of trouble. You need to check as much as possible prior to the purchase, so test-drive it yourself, or try to take along someone who knows their way around the machine. You must see it in action before money changes hands. It would also be prudent to get some idea of the potential cost of repairs or replacement parts for this particular model.

Listen to the motor running, when idling and when under load; undue noise levels and rattling may indicate worn bearings. Make sure that the blade is running true and that there is no undue play, maybe due to a bent arbor. The table should be flat, and to check this you will need a good straightedge. Make sure there are no cracks in the table, the body or any visible internal mechanisms. There may be obvious signs to indicate a lack of care: maybe large amounts of rust or pitted metal, worn or damaged bolts, possibly even dents. If you buy a machine with obvious faults, there is going to be considerable time and effort required to make it an effective working tool again.

The first checklist below should help you decide whether the saw you are looking at is the one you want. The second list is of items to take along when looking at a used saw. An impressive tool kit, a little knowledge and a confident manner should help your bargaining position.

As with the used-car market, there are bargains to be had if you have the time, inclination and background knowledge to understand what you are buying but remember there is nothing to be gained from buying someone else's problems.

ⓒHECKLIST

Points to note on a second-hand saw

- General condition: are there any visible cracks, rust, dents, etc.?
- Are any parts missing?
- Can any cracks be seen in the internal set-up?
- Are there damaged teeth on the internal rack system?
- Arbor and bearings: Do they run smoothly, without play or obvious wear?
- Motor: Does it run smoothly? Does it struggle under load?
- Is the machine stable?
- Is the table flat?
- Fences: Are they straight? Do they move freely and lock securely?
- Handwheels and power switches: Do they operate well?
- Is the manual supplied?

ⓒHECKLIST

Tools for testing

- Small engineer's square
- Straightedge
- Feeler gauge
- Selection of spanners
- Wood for test pieces
- Push sticks
- Safety glasses
- Hearing protection

1:2 Tablesaw anatomy

This chapter describes those essential parts which, working together in combination, make up a fully functioning tablesaw. The better you understand what the various parts do and how they work, the closer you can come to realizing the full potential of this versatile but basically simple machine.

The parts to be considered in this chapter are:

- power button
- saw table
- throat plate
- riving knife
- blade guard

- mitre gauge
- rip fence
- adjustment wheels
- internal mechanisms

Whichever type of tablesaw you choose, it will have all the above features, though materials, design and quality can differ greatly from one model to another. Blades will be discussed separately in Chapter 1:4.

Anatomy of a cabinet saw

The features shown are common to most tablesaws, though the layout of the controls will vary from one model to another.

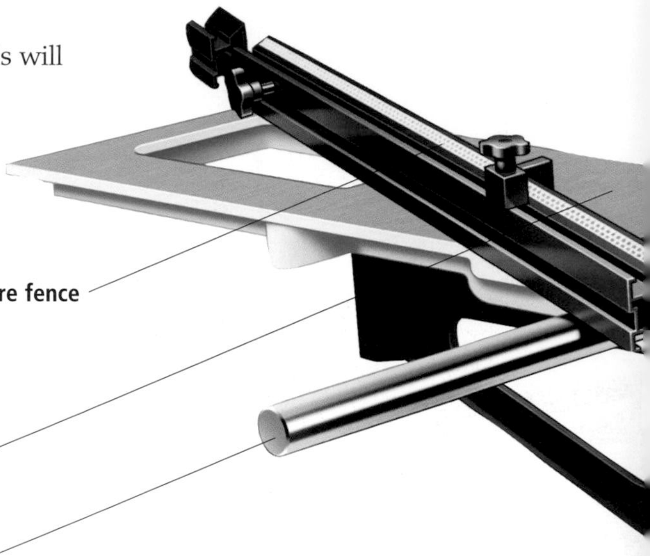

Adjustable mitre fence

Sliding carriage

Sliding carriage rail

Height adjustment wheel

Blade tilt scale

Kick stop

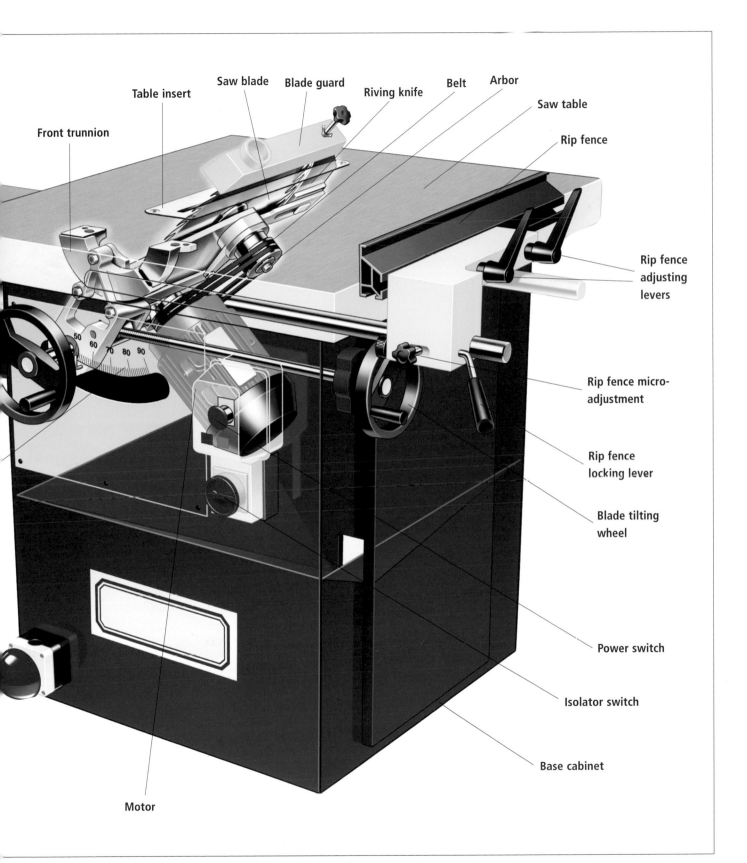

Table insert · Saw blade · Blade guard · Riving knife · Belt · Arbor · Saw table · Front trunnion · Rip fence · Rip fence adjusting levers · Rip fence micro-adjustment · Rip fence locking lever · Blade tilting wheel · Power switch · Isolator switch · Base cabinet · Motor

The power button

The mechanism by which you control the flow of electrical current from source to saw may be a pressure button, a flip-switch or a dial-type switch. It is usually located on the front of the machine, within easy striking distance of the user's knee, so operations can cease in an instant if need be.

Should the power switch be in an awkward position or out of knee-reach, you can make up a simple solution by hinging a small piece of board to the fence rail and fixing a block to it, in line with the stop button. A hole drilled in the board lines up with the 'on' button. This device will leave your hands free to work above the table.

To ensure added safety, some saws may also incorporate a form of power disabling, whereby power is cut off until a key is inserted – particularly useful if curious youngsters may be lurking. The downside, of course, is that you are bound to lose the key, so spares are a necessity.

The switch mechanism itself can be either magnetic or manual. With a magnetic switch the power is maintained by a flow of electricity through the

ABOVE Switching off the saw quickly, without searching for that red button, should become second nature.

KEY POINT

When setting up a tablesaw, you can often choose whether to attach the power button on the left or the right side. If you are right-handed, it is probably a good idea to have the power switch on the left, on the front of the base casing, as most of the operations carried out will be to the left side of the fence and your stance should naturally be on the left-hand side of the saw.

contacts via an electromagnetic relay, which will shut down should there be a power failure, and will then need to be switched back on manually. This type of mechanism is found more commonly on larger table or cabinet saws. A manual switch relies on the constant pressure of the switch mechanism itself, so when power is restored the saw will automatically restart, which can be dangerous. **With this type you must always make a point of switching off manually if the power supply is interrupted.**

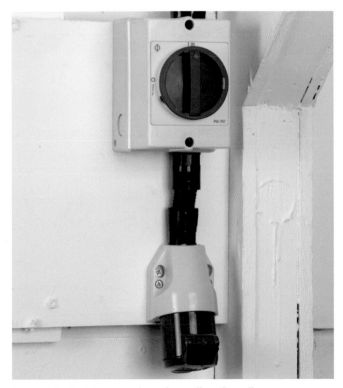

ABOVE An isolator switch at the wall socket allows power to be cut off in an emergency without even approaching the saw.

ABOVE A hinged switch cover within easy striking distance of the user's knee. Paint it a suitably conspicuous colour.

The saw table

ABOVE Cast-iron table on a cabinet saw.

This is the flat surface that supports the workpiece and gives it a smooth passage through the saw blade. Cast table tops are still the preferred option for most workers: heavy cast iron in a workshop, or aluminium alloy for more portable machines.

Flatness, smoothness, stability and durability are the key factors in a saw table. To check for a true and flat surface you will need a good straightedge;

if possible, check it for trueness against another straightedge first. Move it gently over the length and breadth of the table, checking carefully for any abnormalities such as warp, which is common in older machines. Tables can be reground if necessary, and this is less expensive than you may imagine; but a true and well-made table, especially in cast iron, can last for many years and give generations of reliable service.

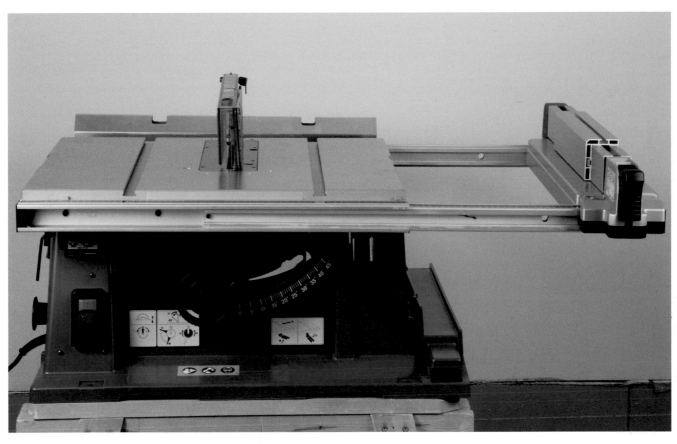

ABOVE Aluminium-alloy table on a portable saw.

(i) KEY POINT

Giving the table top an occasional coat of wax – furniture, floor or car wax, or perhaps some other, custom-made product – will greatly lessen friction, allowing the work to move smoothly and easily across the table and through the blade. It is wise to buff the surface to ensure there is no build-up of wax over time, perhaps cleaning it occasionally with a mild solvent.

Talcum powder reputedly has the same effect, but with the added advantage of filling up open pores in the cast surface – though I have not tried this myself, and there might be a risk of clogging up moving parts unless due care is taken.

ABOVE Checking the table for flatness using a straightedge.

31

ABOVE An extension table or 'wing' fixed to the main table.

Extending the workspace

As you improve your skills, and your projects become more complex and demanding, it is more than likely that you will need to increase your machine's capacity with 'wing' extension tables. In addition to allowing you to use longer and wider stock, these extensions provide more stability and thereby greatly increase safety; manoeuvring large boards on a small table can be quite hazardous. Extension tables can be purchased, but it is also perfectly feasible to make your own.

ABOVE An auxiliary mitre fence in hardwood, raised slightly above the table to allow dust to escape.

Another possibility is a sliding table affixed to the left side of the saw table, as described on page 21, with a rail and guide system to provide easier, more accurate and safer cutting. The cost may be prohibitive, but imaginative woodworkers have devised ingenious home-made substitutes. Less expensive alternatives include fitting an extension bar to the mitre gauge (a length of hardwood or laminate will suffice), or making a crosscutting jig or sled as described on pages 140–9.

The throat plate

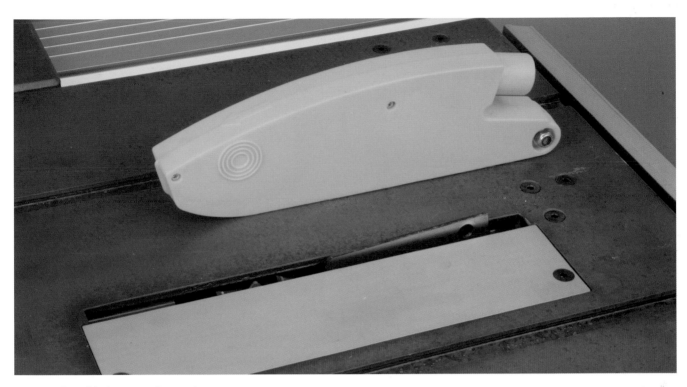

ABOVE The table insert or throat plate.

Lying flush with the table top is the throat plate or table insert, through which the saw blade rises and falls. It is made from soft, non-ferrous material so as not to cause sparks, ignition or serious damage if it should contact the blade. Often the height can be adjusted by inset screws in order to level it perfectly to the table. Removing the insert gives access to the arbor through the throat, allowing blade changing and adjustment to the riving-knife bracket.

A slot in the throat plate permits the blade and riving knife to ascend through the opening; the slot is large enough to allow for blade tilting. For some applications, however, you may prefer to make your own zero-tolerance throat plate – that is, one which leaves no space between itself and the blade, thus reducing or even eliminating ragged edges on the work. This is illustrated on page 59.

ABOVE On this model, tiny grub screws on the shoulder of the throat allow the depth of the insert to be adjusted.

KEY POINT

Before you take out the throat plate, disconnect the power supply; don't take chances.

The riving knife

ABOVE Sitting directly behind the blade, the riving knife or splitter is an essential safety component.

The small steel scythe-like feature which sits up at the rear of the saw blade is one of the prime safety features on the tablesaw. It is called the riving knife, or, in the US, the splitter – which fairly accurately describes its function.

When a piece of timber is ripped (cut along the grain), there will be a natural tendency for the saw cut in the wood to close up as it passes through, so as to pinch the blade. Consequently, the teeth on the far side of the blade, which are rising through the table insert, can flip the wood back up with great force towards the operator, a situation known as 'kickback'. The riving knife, if it is set correctly, will go a long way to eliminate this serious danger.

A well-designed riving knife should have a chamfered leading edge of the same thickness as the saw blade or thicker, but slightly less than the width of the saw cut or 'kerf'. When correctly positioned, it should follow the curve of the blade.

In theory, wood will only pinch when being cut with the grain, because of pressures released as the timber is cut. When cutting across the grain, the wood fibres are being severed, so there ought to be no need to rely on a riving knife, but in reality it will always be safer to make use of the facility. Timber is liable to be skewed – that is, moved out of alignment with the blade – at any time during any cut, so kickback is always a possibility.

⊙ KEY POINT

In order to be effective, the riving knife should sit no more than ⅜–½in (10–12mm) behind the saw blade, and should rise and fall in unison with it. For blades greater than 24in (600mm) diameter the knife should rise to at least 9in (230mm) above the table.

The knife is often mounted on a bracket located underneath the table, and in turn the blade guard is often fixed to the riving-knife mechanism.

On saws made in the US, and very occasionally on European saws, you can see, mounted alongside the splitter, a set of anti-kickback pawls. Their function is to dig into the wood and prevent it being thrown back should kickback occur, either through misalignment of splitter and blade, or through use of an undersized splitter.

ABOVE The riving knife closely follows the arc of the blade.

ABOVE The slots or notches in the top of the riving knife are attachment points for the blade guard.

The blade guard

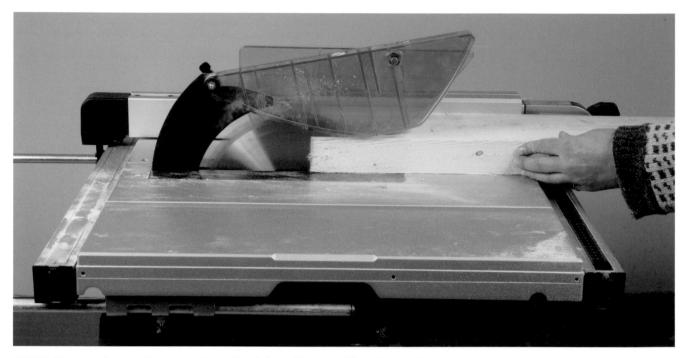

ABOVE The guard must offer protection to hands from above and from both sides.

It is the job of the blade guard to act as a barrier between the saw blade and the operator, while permitting access to the workpiece, and to prevent anything other than the timber from passing through the blade.

Wood chips and sawdust thrown up by the blade are also contained by the guard to some extent, though this function is increased immeasurably by attaching some kind of extraction device to the guard, which should have a dedicated extraction port. Though there are specially designed units to fulfil this function, any half-decent domestic vacuum cleaner will do the job.

Guards really are a necessity, and a good guard which is both protective and gives good visibility is certainly a worthwhile investment. Unfortunately not all guards fit these criteria, but even a poor guard is

ABOVE A domestic vacuum cleaner can deal with above-table dust extraction; use tape if necessary to secure the connection.

better than none at all. Shop around for a durable guard that does not interfere with the passage of the work, or with visibility. Some home-made jigs may need their own guard, which can be quickly made with some clear acrylic or polycarbonate sheet and a little ingenuity (some examples can be seen on pages 168–9).

(KEY POINT

It is most important to remember that no guard will give totally risk-free cutting, so be constantly aware of the potential for damage should contact occur between blade and user. Stay vigilant at all times when using a tablesaw, and keep hands, hair, clothing and everything else as far from the blade as is reasonably possible.

(FOCUS ON:

Blade safety

There are times when a blade guard might seem to obstruct and limit certain types of saw cuts, and in some older books you may see references to techniques which require the guard to be removed. It is, however, becoming widely recognized that to work without any kind of guard is unacceptable, and the stringent European guidelines on health and safety are beginning to be adopted in the US also.

Removing the standard guard to increase the saw's capability may be acceptable in some situations, but only if adequate alternative safety measures are used. These might include:

- an overarm or tunnel guard (such as those described overleaf) or
- a home-made blade guard or covered jig specific to a certain saw cut;

and, *in addition to these*, safety accessories such as push sticks, featherboards and hold-downs.

The operator should be protected from the blade both from above and from either side of it. If you find yourself in a situation where this is not the case, stop and look for a better way.

ABOVE A rebate like this cannot be cut with a standard blade guard in place, so alternative safety measures must be adopted.

ABOVE A small, straight-edged block of wood clamped to the rip fence acts as a simple hold-down (the blade guard has been removed for clarity).

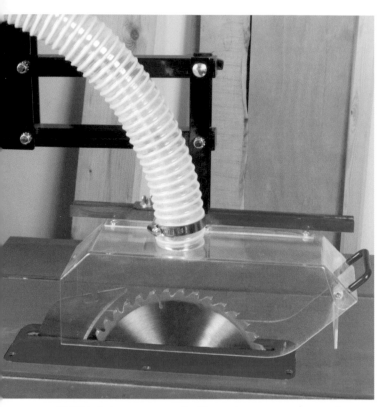

ABOVE An overarm guard will permit a greater range of cuts than the standard blade guard; this particular model is known as a crown guard.

The crown guard

This type of overarm guard differs from the standard blade guard in that it is not fixed to the riving-knife bracket, but extends over the table on its own arm. It can therefore be placed above the blade and the work, in order to allow non-through cuts – that is, cuts which do not go all the way through the board – or other cuts which would not be possible using the standard guard.

When attempting cuts of this nature, the riving knife must be lowered so as to be at the same height as the top of the blade or just below, so the work can pass through smoothly. It is always necessary to be extra-cautious when making these kinds of cuts, using additional safety devices such as hold-downs, featherboards and push sticks.

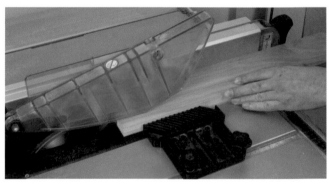

ABOVE A fingerboard or featherboard holds the workpiece against the rip fence.

ABOVE Push sticks in action. The long-nosed one keeps the workpiece flat to the table, while the other presses it firmly against the fence.

The SUVA guard

This is a variety of crown guard that is not fixed to the arbor bracket or riving knife. It is manoeuvred to the work by pulling it across on a sliding bar (or bars) from its fixed bracket mounted on the side of the table. It provides more scope for varying the cuts, but again every effort must be made to ensure that the blade is not exposed in any way to the user. The same applies to crown guards which are in a fixed position above the blade, held in place by way of a heavy-duty extending bar fixed to the table, or indeed to ceiling- or roof-mounted crown guards which are lowered to just above the blade from their fixed position above.

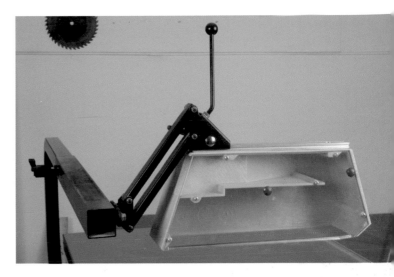

ABOVE The SUVA guard is a form crown guard mounted on an adjustable bracket.

The Shaw guard

This uses a system of adjustable rods affixed with pressure-pad-style blocks from above and to the side of the workpiece. They can be adjusted to form a tunnel for the work to pass through. The guard may be fixed to the rip fence or to the table. A home-made version could easily be devised. The not uncontroversial subject of guards will be looked at in more detail in Chapter 2:1.

ABOVE The Shaw guard in use.

The mitre gauge

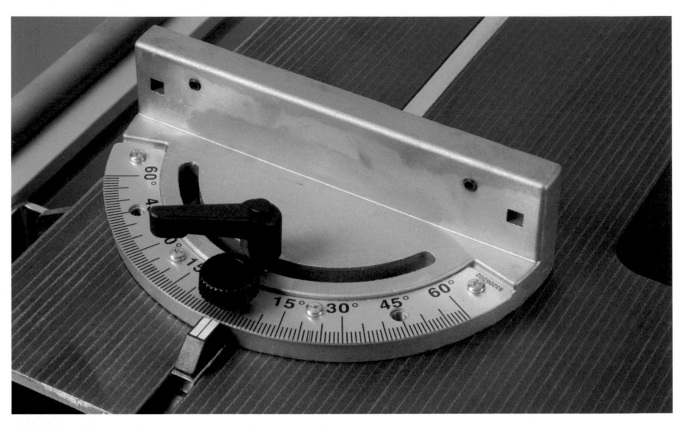

ABOVE The mitre gauge, for accurate crosscutting at any angle.

When you want to cut across a piece of timber – that is, through the grain and not along the length of it – the mitre gauge will help to guide the work through the blade at a suitable angle. It consists of an adjustable protractor head with a face to support the work. Cutting angles from 30° up to 90° can be locked onto as the gauge pivots to the left or right, but it is most often used at 90° for a right-angled pass or 45° for a mitre. Lockable stops are often provided for these two angles so they can be speedily located whenever you need them.

Quality of design and material will vary, but the gauge will often be made from either soft cast metal or a tough polymerized substance; in my experience, the heavier and sturdier, the better.

ABOVE Crosscutting at an angle, using the mitre gauge.

You may want to add your own auxiliary fence to the face of the mitre gauge; this will give you increased efficiency by offering a longer and more stable surface to work from. It is simple enough to screw or bolt a length of hardwood or laminated board to the face of the existing gauge, which will most likely already have slots pre-drilled for this purpose.

ABOVE Extending the workface of the mitre gauge by screwing or bolting on a length of straight-grained hardwood will aid accurate crosscutting.

ABOVE Once the mitre gauge has been set up correctly, the locking stops will readily locate preset angles such as 90°.

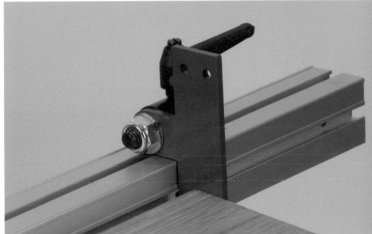

ABOVE A flip-down stop attached to an extended mitre-gauge fence ensures repeated cuts of consistent length.

The mitre gauge has a tongue, known as the mitre bar, which slides back and forth along the table in parallel grooves or trenches accurately machined on either side of the blade.

The flip-down stop

The adjustable stop fitted to some mitre gauges is a useful device when a series of repetitive cuts is to be made. Simply move the stop on the mitre fence to the desired distance from the blade, then lock in place. Resting each successive piece against the stop will give the same length time and again.

⟮TECHNIQUE:

Using double-sided tape, affix some fine abrasive paper to the mitre-gauge fence. This will grip the workpiece, reducing the risk of unwanted movement.

A home-made crosscut sled, described on pages 140–9, can be used instead of a mitre gauge for many crosscutting operations.

The rip fence

This runs parallel to the blade, and serves to guide wood which is being cut along the grain, or 'ripped', to the desired width. The width is determined by the distance between the inner edge of the saw blade and the rip fence.

It is the length of the front and rear rails which determines the actual width-cutting capacity of the saw, and the rails can often be moved to the left or right of the table to extend the cutting possibilities.

ABOVE A standard ripping cut in progress.

ABOVE Locked down firmly to the table and parallel to the blade, the rip fence will be in constant use.

ABOVE The extension rails on this saw are to the right of the blade, but can be readily moved to the other side.

The rip fence must be square to the saw table, sliding easily on the guide rails at the front and sometimes also the rear of the table, and locking into position with a clamping lever or knob. A scale on the front rail, when aligned correctly, will give a clear reading of the distance between the cutting edge of the blade nearest to the fence and the fence itself. If you switch to a blade of different thickness, the zero marker on the scale will need to be reset, but this is simple enough. Occasionally, set within the fence head there may be a micro-gauge for fine adjustment.

(KEY POINT

Because of the possibility of wood movement during the ripping process, some rip fences have shorter auxiliary fences bolted or screwed to their face side. The short fence can be adjusted so as to end where the saw blade begins its cut. This means the wood will be free to move after being cut, without the pressure build-up which might occur were it tight up against a rip fence.

ABOVE A short auxiliary rip fence.

ABOVE The locking-down lever on the rip fence; the measuring scale on the front rail can also be seen.

ABOVE The micro-gauge for accurate measurement of the fence position.

Adjustment wheels

ABOVE Handwheels for blade rise and fall on the front of the saw, and for blade tilt on the side.

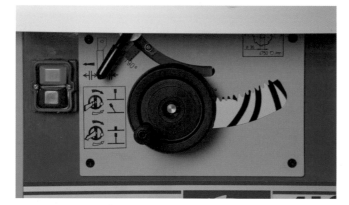

ABOVE This model has a single wheel for both height and tilt adjustment.

The adjustment wheels, which are common to all tablesaws, cause the saw blade to rise or fall, and to tilt between the angles of 90° and 45°.

Most commonly, the set-up comprises two handwheels on the front of the machine: a blade-raising wheel and a blade-tilting wheel. Sometimes the tilt wheel will be found to the side, and its corresponding degree gauge to the front of the saw will give a reasonably accurate indication of the angle. Occasionally a single wheel may complete both operations, pushing in or pulling out to lock into a different mode. On some models a locking device, usually centred within the handwheel, allows the chosen setting to be held solidly in place.

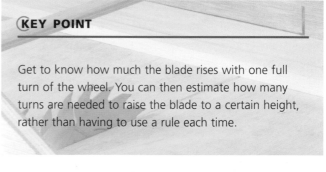

KEY POINT

Get to know how much the blade rises with one full turn of the wheel. You can then estimate how many turns are needed to raise the blade to a certain height, rather than having to use a rule each time.

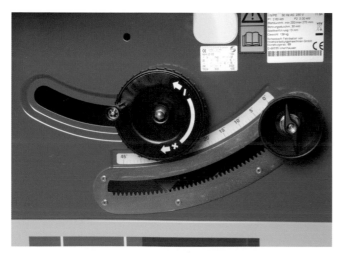

ABOVE A saw with both adjusting wheels on the front.

ABOVE The locking nut centred within the blade-tilt wheel.

ⓕ FOCUS ON:

Blade adjustment

To make sure the blade is set correctly, raise it vertically to its full height and use an engineer's square or a combination square against the table. Place the square solidly to the table and lightly up against the *face* of the saw blade, *not* against the teeth. If blade and square do not match accurately, adjust the wheel accordingly, and mark this angle on the gauge as 90°.

It is also wise to check the blade angles when cutting bevels if you want really accurate work, though often the commonly used angles of 45° and 90° have built-in stops on the arbor arm for quick and easy locating.

Constant tilting of the blade may eventually cause the stabilizing mechanisms within the arbor cradle to move out of line, and even buckle. Added to this, because both handwheels run on a rack-and-pinion system, a build-up of dust, pitch and grease between the teeth will in time impact and harden, causing the gears to stick and even stress, throwing the whole assembly out of line. It is important, therefore, to get under your machine and give it a good clean every so often, and at the same time check for alignment. A good water-based solvent and a small wire brush will keep things neat and tidy. When dry, spray with a light engine oil. Once you have cleaned and set it properly, and can see and feel the difference, you will work more confidently and efficiently.

ABOVE The arbor cradle, holding the motor and the rack-and-pinion system for the handwheels; some pitch build-up can be seen here.

ABOVE Using a combination square to check that the blade is set at 90° to the table.

ⓚ KEY POINT

Jig making is a very good way to familiarize yourself with your machine, while at the same time making many tasks easier, quicker and less frustrating, and saving wear and tear on the saw itself. The bevelling jig on pages 164–5, for example, will allow you to leave the saw set up in the correct position, with everything locked down into place, moving only the jig.

Internal mechanisms

What goes on below the table needs to be set up and maintained with the same diligence as the workings above the table, so it is worthwhile familiarizing yourself with your tablesaw's inner mechanisms.

Some people take readily to this kind of activity, relishing the prospect of loosening and retightening bolts, moving bits around in order to see what they do and generally getting dirt under their fingernails; others prefer not to know what is happening in that dark, dirty, noisy netherworld. However, knowledge is power, so better to bite the bullet and get to know the basics at least.

The blade is mounted on a spindle (the arbor), which in turn is driven by the motor, either directly or by a belt-and-pulley system. The arbor sits in an arbor assembly, which includes the rack and pinion or sector gears, by which the blade is raised and lowered. This assemblage, together with the motor, is set within a carriage assembly or cradle, all held in place by the front and rear trunnions, connected together by a set of rails or rods. This set-up in turn allows the arbor cradle to be tilted for angled cuts, again by means of a rack-and-pinion system, as the handwheel turns the worm gear through the arc-shaped trunnion or rack to give the blade tilt.

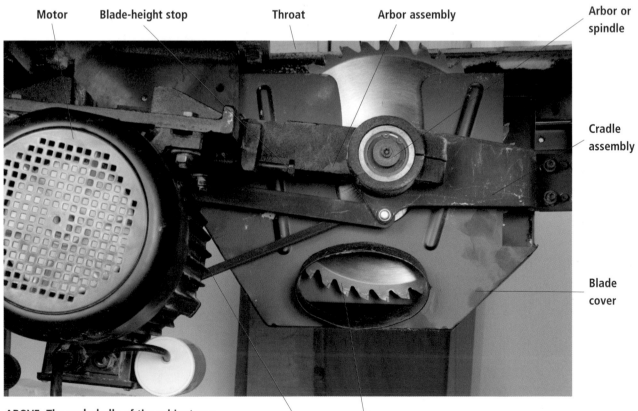

Motor   **Blade-height stop**   **Throat**   **Arbor assembly**   **Arbor or spindle**

Cradle assembly

Blade cover

ABOVE The underbelly of the cabinet saw.

Drive belt   **Saw blade**

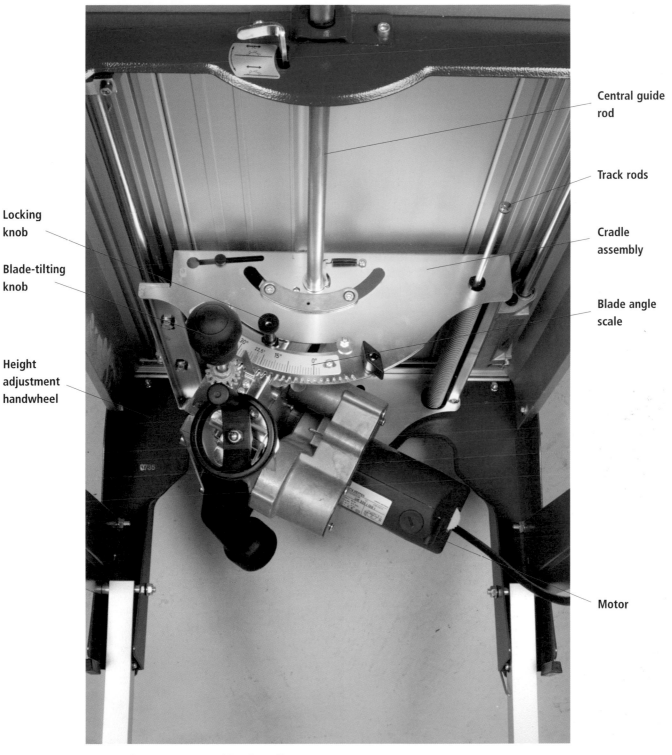

Central guide rod

Track rods

Locking knob

Cradle assembly

Blade-tilting knob

Blade angle scale

Height adjustment handwheel

Motor

ABOVE The carriage assembly of a pull saw.

1:3 Setting up and maintenance

The higher the quality of your tablesaw, the less you should need to work on it in the initial setting-up stage. Nevertheless, this process is both crucial and educational: it will go a long way towards familiarizing you with the workings of the saw and its functions.

The information in this chapter should be read in conjunction with the owner's manual, which will alert you to any peculiarities of your particular model. If you did not get a manual with the saw, it should be available from the manufacturers; you may be able to download it from their website. Alternatively, there are reference books which you may find a little more user-friendly than the standard operating manuals.

Take the setting-up process seriously: it will give you more confidence, and it will lead to safer working practices and more accurate work. For all these reasons it is well worth the initial effort.

Cleaning and lubricating

ABOVE An old paintbrush and methylated spirit (denatured alcohol) will help clean up moving parts before lubrication.

With the saw unplugged from any power source, and the blade removed, first give the insides a good clean, initially with a vacuum cleaner if there appears to be dust present. If there is an abundance of grease, use a degreasing compound or a non-flammable solvent to remove it. An old paintbrush or toothbrush and a rag are ideal for this operation. If grease is left in place it will quickly attract sawdust, and when mixed with the pitch from worked timber this will eventually harden and damage the internal workings of your machine.

When cleaned, you can apply a light, dry lubricant or furniture wax to the moving parts, especially the blade raising and tilting mechanisms. If waxing, apply lightly with a brush so as not to attract excess dust, and do not buff.

In most new models the bearings will be inaccessible, being housed in a sealed unit. If, however, there is a small port to allow for some lubrication, a light machine oil in small quantities, twice a year, should suffice.

ABOVE New saws generally come with a great deal of grease on board, ready to attract sawdust and associated debris.

ABOVE Degreasing compound applied with an old paintbrush will remove dirt build-up on internal components.

Checks and adjustments

The saw will only function efficiently if all the parts are running true and accurately adjusted to one another. You cannot take this for granted: it is up to you to check and make any necessary adjustments. I strongly recommend that you carry out these checks in a fixed and methodical order; otherwise, if the saw is not producing accurate results, it can be very difficult to diagnose where the problem lies. The order I suggest is set out in the panel.

KEY POINT

The more care you take over the initial set-up and subsequent routine maintenance, the longer the saw will work for you and the more likely it is to give the results you want. We all know this, but putting it into practice requires regular effort.

CHECKLIST

Tablesaw maintenance

1 Arbor and bearings
Arbor must turn smoothly with no play or undue resistance

2 Belt alignment
Pulleys must be aligned so drive belt runs straight

3 Alignment of arbor, blade and mitre slots
Saw blade and mitre slots must be exactly parallel

4 Blade angle
Blade must be vertical when tilt scale reads 90°

5 Flatness of table and throat plate
Table must be free of warping, bumps or large depressions

6 Alignment of riving knife
Riving knife must be correctly located behind the blade

7 Alignment of blade guard
Whatever kind of guard is fitted, it must provide access for the work and protection for the hands

8 Alignment of rip fence
Fence must be upright, parallel to mitre slots and blade

9 Alignment of mitre gauge
Mitre gauge must be accurately set and free from play

10 Checking for arbor runout
If all else fails, distortion of the arbor may be suspected

ABOVE Using a feeler gauge to check for arbor runout (see page 66).

1 Arbor and bearings

Take a good look at the blade arbor or spindle, with the saw unplugged and the blade removed. It should be smooth to the touch. Anything that might interfere with the even running of the blade must be dealt with. Small imperfections such as burrs or gouges can be cleaned up with a light, fine filing, but if there is any serious deficiency in the arbor – for instance, any sign of buckling – then the component will have to be replaced. In principle there should be no such problems with new saws, but it is wise to check just in case.

The arbor should run smoothly on well-functioning bearings. With the drive belt removed, try turning the arbor by hand, feeling for any undue resistance. Try also moving the arbor up and down: there really should be no play at all. If either resistance or play are suspected, then the bearings are probably worn or faulty, and must be replaced. If the saw is no longer under warranty, you will have to return it to the manufacturer or take it to a repair shop. Don't attempt to do the job yourself unless you have the correct tools and some specialist know-how.

ABOVE Checking for undue play in the arbor.

2 Belt alignment

The belt or belts from the arbor pulley to the motor-shaft pulley must run smoothly. The belt should be of the correct size to fit the valley of the pulley wheels snugly, and the pulley wheels themselves must be aligned to each other so that a straightedge placed along the face of one will rest on the face of the other. If the wheels are out of line the belt will not run true, and there will be excessive vibration and excess wear and tear on the belt. A set screw in the motor-shaft pulley can be loosened and the appropriate adjustment made to the pulley, followed by re-tightening of the set screw.

ABOVE The pulley wheel on the arbor is driven by a V-belt (arrowed) from the motor.

ⒻFOCUS ON:

Belt types

The belt on a modern saw is likely to be a V-belt, and must be replaced when worn with a matching belt. If your machine has more than one belt attached, all should be replaced at the same time – even if only one is worn – in order to spread the tension and load evenly.

Some operators claim that other types of belt – such as grooved belts, or segmented belts – provide a more efficient transmission of power with less likelihood of misshaping due to wear.

ABOVE A segmented belt is said to give more efficient power transmission.

ABOVE **A good straightedge will show up an uneven surface.**

ABOVE **Light filing may take out small imperfections.**

ABOVE **A mild abrasive, such as emery cloth or a powdered abrasive, will suffice for minor surface maintenance.**

ABOVE **A diamond sharpening stone can help flatten out bumps and small hollows.**

5 Flatness of table and throat plate

A flat table is essential, being the point of reference for all your work, and the datum from which the alignment of the other components is taken. Using a good-quality straightedge, long enough to reach across the table top, check from corner to corner and from side to side over the length of the table, looking for imperfections such as bumps, hollows or twisting.

Small imperfections can be got rid of easily enough with gentle abrasion – either light filing or rubbing with emery cloth. More stubborn anomalies may need grinding with a coarse diamond stone, or perhaps even a power sander or power grinder. Follow up any serious grinding with lighter abrasion to achieve a smooth finish. Small hollows may not matter, given that in all probability the wood will straddle the hollow. If the depression is wide enough to affect the work, then it may be time to change the table or the saw.

ABOVE Testing for flatness with winding sticks.

It is surprising just how much a cast table can move out of true. Aluminium is especially susceptible, although cast iron is certainly not exempt. Should a table be out of true due to twist, checking diagonally from corner to corner with a straightedge will show up the fault. Another method is to use winding sticks, as when testing for twist in a length of wood. Two pieces of wood with flat, parallel sides, at least as long as the width of the table top, are laid on opposite ends of the table and viewed head on; any deviation between the two sticks will quickly become apparent as you sight across them.

It is possible to correct any twist by applying shims or thin washers between the table top and the cabinet and retightening the lock-down bolts, in order to raise up a section of the table.

ABOVE Shimming the table to correct for twist.

Extension tables

Extension tables bolted to the main table will need some manoeuvring to ensure that they sit on the same plane. Use a straightedge to check. Make sure the joint between the tables is clean, and if necessary add a shim while the two tables are loosely bolted together. The shim should be placed between the tables before tightening up, and with a little luck the two tables should marry up and be perfectly flush.

A supporting table to the rear of the main table, known as an outfeed support, can be fixed or free-standing, but should not interfere with or add stresses to the main table. Set the outfeed table marginally below the saw table, allowing for some movement from vibration, which may raise it slightly. This table must be stable and sturdy enough for the workload involved.

ABOVE These tables are level.

ABOVE A fixed outfeed table (seen at left) makes life easier when working with longer stock.

ABOVE The gap under the straightedge here shows that the main table and extension are not in line.

ABOVE Another example of outfeed support at the rear of a portable or site saw.

The throat plate

The saw should never run without the throat plate or table insert in place. The plate should sit firmly in place and flush to the table top. Metal ones usually have a set of small levelling screws for fine adjusting.

The throat opening is wide enough to allow the blade to tilt to 45° for a bevel cut. Unfortunately, this wide opening also allows slivers of wood to become wedged in the gap, often being thrown back out with some force. For this reason it is usual to make your own insert, which supports the timber right up to the side of the blade when the blade is in the upright position. If you prefer, custom-made table insert blanks can be purchased for most saws.

To make your own, scribe around the existing insert, fingerholes and all, onto a piece of hardwood or good-quality ply, prepared to the same thickness as the original. With the saw blade fully retracted and the power off, shape the insert to fit the opening; a small chamfer along the bottom edge will help it go in. When the fit is right, use strong adhesive tape to fix it to the table. (You can use clamps if you are sure they will not foul the blade.) Then switch on the power, allow the blade to reach full speed, and, with your hands well out of the way, slowly raise it to its full extent, to form a slot which fits the blade exactly.

This so-called 'zero-tolerance' plate improves safety and also prevents to a large extent the tear-out or fraying which is common with unsupported cuts. Bevel cuts cannot be performed with this type of throat plate in place; many woodworkers prefer to leave the saw blade set at 90°, and either make or buy a jig for angled cuts. A solid 45° jig, as described on pages 164–5, will serve for the most frequently required bevel cut; a more sophisticated adjustable jig can be constructed later if required.

ABOVE A levelling screw for adjusting the throat plate flush with the table top.

ABOVE Using the throat plate as a template, mark and cut out the zero-tolerance insert precisely.

ABOVE A zero-tolerance throat plate made from plywood.

6 Alignment of riving knife

This essential piece of safety apparatus must be aligned correctly behind the saw blade in order to prevent kickback, as previously discussed. Usually the centres of both should line up, though it is also possible to align the knife with either face of the saw blade. For example, should you wish the knife to keep the work pressed against the rip fence as it passes, then it can be set flush with the side of the saw blade facing the fence. Check the alignment by laying a straightedge across from the face of the saw blade (between the teeth) to the face of the riving knife.

Set the riving knife to ⅜–½in (10–12mm) behind the blade, not more. It should not be removed for cutting, even when the blade is securely guarded and good-quality jigs are being used. If the blade guard has to be removed for certain non-through cuts, the riving knife should be lowered to the same height as the blade or just below, but complete removal is not an option. For some purposes you might need to modify the riving knife or change it for one of a more appropriate model.

KEY POINT

Remember that the blade guard must never be removed unless adequate alternative safety precautions are in place, as described on page 39 and elsewhere.

ABOVE The riving knife correctly adjusted to the same height as the blade.

ABOVE Using a straightedge to align the riving knife or splitter with the saw blade.

7 Alignment of blade guard

When the guard is in place it should cover the saw blade whilst allowing easy, unimpeded access for the workpiece. It should allow full access for the push sticks you will be using, and also allow for the use of hold-downs to keep the work in place. It should not impede access to the blade – while the machine is switched off and unplugged – for changing it or measuring up against it. Removing it when necessary should be a quick and simple task. Visibility through the guard is very useful; just a few models are made of some type of transparent polymer, offering clear visibility provided the view is not hampered by the manufacturer's logo or a safety sticker.

Very few guards meet all these criteria. Moreover, since most are attached to the blade arbor, it is impossible to make hidden cuts such as rebates or housings without removing the guard – thereby contravening health and safety regulations, which are applicable in law. The standard guard and riving knife may also prevent the use of devices such as a crosscut sled or a tenoning jig. This means that changes may need to be made in order to increase the versatility of the saw while keeping the operations safe.

If you are unhappy with the guard supplied by the manufacturer, consider buying another model that fits your needs better. Unfortunately this can be expensive, especially if you decide on a table-mounted crown guard. These are often large, bulky affairs, but a good-quality model should give you the freedom to make any cuts you require, safely.

If you make your own jigs for the majority of the operations employed on the tablesaw, you can devise home-made guards which will give suitable protection without interfering with the cutting procedure, as described in Part 3.

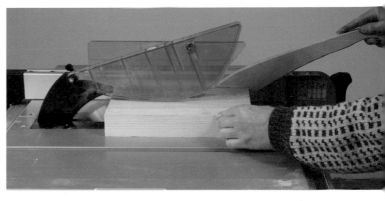

ABOVE The blade guard correctly positioned, protecting the user from contact with the blade while leaving sufficient access for the workpiece.

ABOVE This guard can be removed by means of a simple locking lever. It features a basic but effective dust-extraction facility, and leaves room for a hold-down unit.

ABOVE The inevitable safety sticker on the blade guard does little to improve visibility.

ABOVE An effective method of aligning the rip fence to the mitre slots.

8 Alignment of rip fence

For clean cutting of timber, the rip fence must have a flat surface and be parallel to the mitre slots and saw blade, while standing at a square 90° to the table. If not, you will encounter an array of unwelcome problems, from unsightly burn marks on the timber, to wood jamming between blade and fence – a potentially dangerous situation if the wood is flung back towards you.

Only when you are sure that the blade is aligned parallel to the mitre slots (see section 3 above) should you think about aligning the rip fence so it is parallel with both of them. One method is to use a straightedge clamped parallel to the mitre

ABOVE Using a square to check that the face of the fence is at exactly 90° to the table.

slots, or to a correctly set saw blade. Alternatively, a dial indicator, affixed to the mitre gauge and lined up with first one end of the fence then the other, allows any deviation to be precisely measured. This sophisticated engineering device is relatively inexpensive and very useful for woodworking machinery. The base of the instrument is magnetized and fixes securely to iron or steel surfaces. Adjustments will usually be made via Allen screws or bolts on the top or side of the rip fence.

ABOVE A dial indicator will show the alignment of the fence very precisely.

ABOVE This particular rip fence is adjusting by loosening the Allen nuts.

(FOCUS ON:

Auxiliary fences

The length of the rip fence – or rather, the amount of it that is used – is important. A stable piece of material, such as crosscut timber, medium-density fibreboard (MDF), plywood or chipboard, can travel the whole length of the rip fence for a precise cut. When ripping solid timber, however, there is likely to be some movement or distortion in the material as the cut is made. The danger of the timber pinching on the rear teeth of the saw blade is lessened greatly by the use of a riving knife or splitter, and also by shortening the rip fence so that as the wood leaves the blade it is no longer in contact with the fence. If your fence is not adjustable in this way, you can fit a short extra face to it, carefully adjusted to line up with the front of the saw blade, so that as the wood comes off the blade there is a space between it and the fence proper.

ABOVE An additional shortened fence attached to the face of the rip fence gives room for the workpiece to move as it passes through the blade (see page 119).

Check the overall flatness of your rip fence with a straightedge. Some unevenness is not uncommon with older, stamped-steel models. Adding a home-made auxiliary fence, shimmed as necessary to give a fully flat surface, is much cheaper than buying a new rip fence.

ABOVE Using the fine-adjustment screw stop to set the mitre gauge at 90° to the mitre slots.

9 Alignment of mitre gauge

Because the mitre gauge comes in for heavy use, it must be accurately set and regularly checked to make sure it has not moved out of true. It must fit snugly into the mitre slots milled in the table top, and, when set to the 90° mark on the adjustable protractor head, it must run at an exact right angle to the mitre slots and to the saw blade.

If there happens to be any looseness between gauge and slots, a good tip for improving the fit is to take a punch or a cold chisel and make a series of punches or grooves in the sides of the mitre bar at regular intervals of 2in (50mm); this will provide

a tighter fit in the short term, but if the gauge has daily, rigorous use this solution will be only temporary. Some gauges have small Allen screws or grub screws embedded in the side of the mitre bar, which can be let out slightly to give a secure fit.

Adjust the gauge at 90° to the saw blade, as accurately as you can by sight, then make a cut in a piece of scrap wood. Flip one of the cut pieces and butt it up to the other on a flat surface, and any discrepancy will be easy to see. Merely readjust the gauge by trial and error until it gives an accurate result. For efficient, speedy adjustment there is often

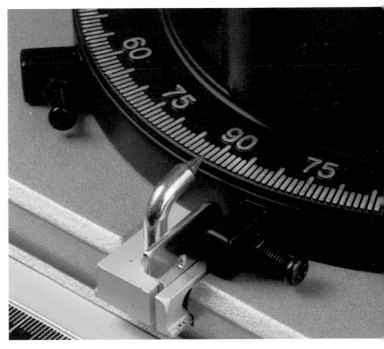

BELOW Once the mitre fence is producing an accurate right angle, set the stop to 90°.

ABOVE A series of punch holes evenly spaced along the mitre bar will correct any sloppiness in the fit.

a stop at both the 90° and 45° indicators on the measurement gauge. A set screw which presses up to each stop will allow for automatic lining up with these commonly used angles; when the gauge is set correctly, tighten the screws in place.

I think it worthwhile to add an auxiliary fence to the mitre gauge immediately, to increase its range and versatility. This can be a sturdy length of stable hardwood no less than 1in (25mm) thick, which extends beyond the outboard side of the fence for at least 6in (150mm). Most likely the gauge will already have pre-drilled locating holes for it.

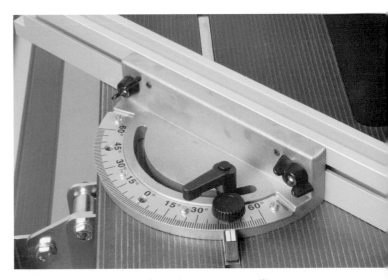

ABOVE An auxiliary mitre fence increases versatility.

10 Checking for arbor runout

The rotation of the arbor, and consequently the saw blade, should be close to perfect. If the saw cuts you make show anything other than a clean and even finish, even after you have made all the adjustments described above, this is most likely a symptom of uneven rotation, or runout – but do double-check to eliminate other causes before assuming that this is the case.

If the problem is with the arbor itself, you can really only find out by examining in detail the rotation of the flange which is mounted on the arbor; this is often fixed, but not always. Measuring the evenness of the rotation is best carried out with a dial indicator contacting the arbor flange. Make a chalk mark at the starting point, rotate the arbor one full cycle and read the amount of deviation on the dial.

A more home-grown solution is to clamp a sturdy pointed indicator to the mitre gauge, making sure it extends to the arbor flange, rotate the apparatus full circle and pinpoint any deviation with the use of feeler gauges.

A deviation of no more than 0.001in (0.025mm) is acceptable; any more than this will cause vibration that will adversely affect cutting. In this case, the arbor and flange will need to be removed and taken to a machine shop to be re-skimmed into true.

ABOVE The arbor and its flange.

ABOVE The dial indicator measures any deviation in the rotation of the arbor flange.

Installing the tablesaw

Location

Having assembled your tablesaw, a first and most important step is to find the most efficient location for it within the workshop. The main consideration is to ensure that it has enough space around it; as explained on page 18, an area of 20ft x 12ft 6in (6 x 3.8m) will be enough to handle standard sheet materials. If you expect to use extension tables, make sure enough extra space is allowed for these. You also need to consider the placement of the saw in relation to your:

- emergency or fire exit
- electricity supply
- wood source or timber stack
- light sources
- dust collection or extraction equipment
- other tools and machines.

And it is not a bad idea to have the saw facing the workshop entrance so that unexpected visitors will not take you by surprise.

It is not unusual to find the tablesaw at the heart of a workshop, because it is often at the centre of the woodworking process: timber will need to be dimensioned before most other operations can be carried out, so the tablesaw will be the first link in the production chain.

KEY POINT

If the saw is to be moved regularly, you could mark out its position on the floor with tape or paint. Thin 'soles' of wood or plastic will protect the floor from scratching.

In smaller spaces it may be easier to use a portable saw; this can easily be moved to free up space for other types of working, and, when the weather allows, use of outside space is an option.

Stability

A stable machine, with as little vibration as possible, is essential for safety and accuracy. All four legs or corners of the cabinet should be touching the floor with no movement apparent; small wedges or shims may be needed to secure the saw in the right position. Adjust these carefully, with the aid of a spirit level and straightedge, until you have a stable and level table to work from.

Some machines can be fixed to the floor, and if the floor is solid enough this provides an adequate anchoring point. Placing the machine on a rubberized mat prior to fixing should also help to keep any vibration to a minimum. Supplementary infeed or outfeed tables will contribute to keeping the whole unit stable.

BELOW The castors on two corners of this machine necessitate levelling blocks on the other corners.

Regular maintenance

Initial cleaning and lubrication have already been covered at the beginning of this chapter. Subsequent routine maintenance is largely a matter of keeping up to speed with the regular cleaning of the saw. A vacuum cleaner set to blow rather than suck is a good and quick way to diperse sawdust and loose chippings, both on the inside and outside of the machine, followed by a quick check to ensure that no debris has lodged in any of the important mechanisms, such as the sector gear or trunnions. Should there be any build-up of dust, pitch or grease, a dry solvent or mineral spirits (white spirit) should be applied, either with a cloth or an old toothbrush, or with steel wool if necessary. Use light machine oil or spray lubricant in the places recommended by the tablesaw manufacturer.

KEY POINT

Keeping on top of basic lubrication and maintenance is really not a very demanding task, and it will increase the life expectancy of your machine considerably. The best way to ensure that nothing gets missed is to keep a log. For those with a methodical mind this will not be a problem; for the rest of us… well, we must endeavour to do our best!

Caring for the saw table

There are good reasons to take the time to maintain the table top of your saw. It is the first point of contact with your work, and a clean, smooth, well-lubricated table will give the work a safer and much

ABOVE Buffing the table after applying wax.

more efficient travel through the cut. Long-term protection from rust is essential, too. At least a couple of times a year, or whenever you feel resistance when passing the workpiece through the machine, take time out to treat the table using the following routine.

First give the table a clean with mineral spirits, using medium-grade steel wool if necessary to remove any rust spots or pitch build-up. An all-over thin coat of wax can then be applied, left to dry for a while, then buffed off. Use a good-quality machine or furniture wax, but not floor wax or silicone-based products. This will provide adequate lubrication without staining the wood. The same process can be carried out on extension tables if appropriate, on the guide rails, and even on the faces of the fences if there are no auxiliary fences attached.

A quick clean and a spray of lubricant into the moving parts of the fence mechanisms will help to keep them fluid and avoid any build-up of deposits.

KEY POINT

A good tip to help combat the insidious problem of condensation is to make up a cardboard cover for the saw, which can be neatly folded and packed away after use.

BELOW A good spray lubricant for moving parts is an essential part of the maintenance regime.

220 x 3.2 x 30 Z 64
n˚ max 10200

1:4 Blades

As all woodworkers know, 'A saw is only as good as its blade.' It is only common sense to choose a saw blade that is the right type for the job, and of good enough quality to cope with the tasks required. There are many blades to choose from, so making an informed choice requires some degree of awareness of the subject.

Never use a blade which is in poor condition or of an inappropriate type: this will undoubtedly result in wasted time and material, and may even compromise your safety.

Three important features are common to all saw blades:

1 the body, or plate
2 the arbor hole, through which the spindle or arbor will fit precisely, with or without the addition of a reducing bush or washer
3 the teeth, available in a number of configurations suitable for a wide range of different tasks.

What to look for in a saw blade

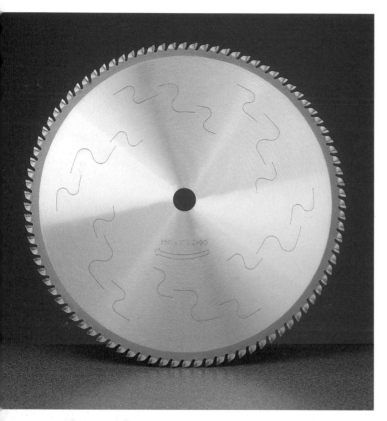

ABOVE A typical circular saw blade with its body, arbor hole and tungsten-carbide-tipped teeth.

1 The body

Tungsten-carbide-tipped (TCT) blades are far and away the preferred choice of woodworkers today. The plate or body is formed from steel or carbon-steel alloy, generally by a laser cutting process, and the carbide teeth are brazed into specially designed 'seats'. The main requirement is for the body to be flat – the flatter the better. Nowadays they are tested at source for flatness by dedicated machinery.

ABOVE Testing a saw blade for flatness.

ABOVE Brazing the tungsten-carbide teeth onto the blade.

Checking for flatness

You would expect a saw blade to be flat when newly purchased, but you should not take it for granted. For a first check, place a straightedge along the surface of the blade – taking care to keep it in between the teeth – hold it up to a good light and check for gaps. A keen eye should be able to spot any deformities, in which case the blade can be changed, or repaired by the manufacturer or a competent saw doctor. A more accurate check can be made with a dial indicator, as described previously on page 66. These can be digital or mechanical, and work within tolerances of 0.001in (1 thousandth of an inch, or 0.025mm). In all likelihood there will be some lack of flatness, or runout, on both arbor and blade, but if kept within a certain tolerance this is acceptable.

There are other ways of checking for flatness in a saw blade, such as using measuring callipers or, not quite as accurately, a measuring stick held firmly against a mitre fence and located on the blade body.

ABOVE Checking for flatness with a dial indicator.

73

FOCUS ON:

Saw blade runout

Remember that the amount of runout will appear larger at the perimeter of the blade than at the arbor flange. If the blade is out of true by more than 0.01in (10 thou, 0.25mm) at its perimeter, then steps should be taken to correct the problem. Anything below this is within acceptable tolerances.

Check that the problem is not with the arbor itself, which should run out at no more than 0.001in (1 thou, 0.025mm). As an approximate example, if the arbor runs out of true by around 0.002in (2 thou, 0.05mm), this translates into a deviation of more than 0.008in (8 thou, 0.2mm) at the edge of an 8in (200mm) blade (the arbor runout is multiplied by the radius of the blade). Add to this figure the runout of the blade (of which there will no doubt be some), and you can get tolerances that are unacceptable for any fine woodworking.

ABOVE This rough check should reveal whether the blade is out of true.

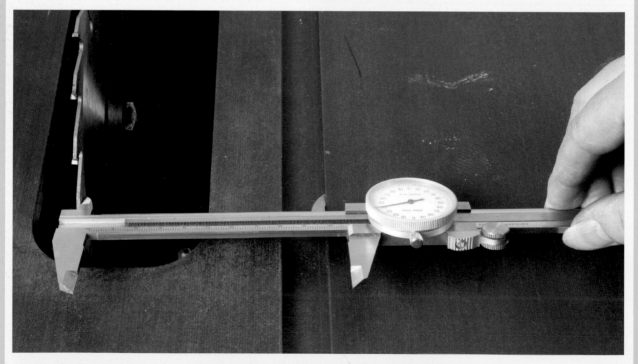

ABOVE Checking for blade runout with dial callipers between the blade and the mitre slot.

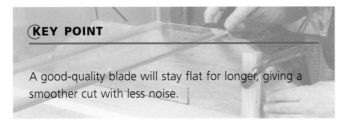

Blade stiffeners

To help stabilize the blade, it is possible to add a flanged collar which is locked in place against the body of the blade by the arbor nut. These precisely engineered washers will add support during a cut, reduce vibration and prolong the life of the blade.

These blade stiffeners, as they are called, are more common in the US than in Europe, and not everyone is convinced of their effectiveness. They may even encourage buckling by adding to the mass of the central part of the blade, so that it heats up much less in use than the perimeter. The depth of cut is also reduced by the radius of the collar. On the whole, it is better if the body of the blade has the thickness required for the job, without relying on any additional support.

2 The arbor hole

Laser-cut holes are preferable to punched-through ones, as the new process causes less stress and distortion. The blade should be a precise fit on the arbor, with no play at all. A separate bush can be inserted into the arbor hole if it differs in size from the arbor; this again must be a very precise fit. Bushes should be easy to get hold of from a power-tool retailer or hardware store.

ABOVE A reducing washer or bush adapts the blade to fit a smaller arbor.

3 The teeth

It is widely acknowledged that the introduction of tungsten carbide has made all other forms of saw teeth virtually redundant. Formed from small blocks of bonded tungsten, carbide and cobalt brazed onto the flat steel plate, the resulting cutting edge is far more effective than the once-common spring-steel blades. Although TCT blades are more expensive, the initial cost is more than offset by their longevity, cutting performance and low maintenance.

It is estimated that a carbide blade will give clean cutting for approximately 50 times longer between sharpenings than a standard steel blade, when used on hardwoods, and up to 400 times longer on man-made materials such as chipboard or MDF. For most general woodwork, one standard combination blade (see page 78) will be sufficient for ripping, crosscutting and sheet materials – which was just not possible prior to the introduction of TCT. Buy a good one – they are not unreasonably expensive.

For more specialized work there are quite a number of blades to choose from: blades of different thicknesses, anti-kickback blades, ultra-fine-finish blades, non-ferrous blades, low-noise blades, and those specially designed for use on laminates and chipboard; but for most purposes one high-quality combination blade will get you a long way.

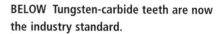

LEFT A good all-purpose blade; this one has 60 teeth, with an alternate top-bevel (ATB) tooth configuration (see page 78).

BELOW Tungsten-carbide teeth are now the industry standard.

Tooth configuration and geometry

There are many variations on tooth angle or profile, suitable for different types of cut on particular materials. It is not essential to know about all of these, but here is a brief summary of the main points for those who are interested.

Pitch, rake or hook

The angle of the tooth as it cuts into the wood is called the pitch, rake or hook. If the face of the tooth is parallel to an imaginary line drawn from the centre of the blade to the tip of the tooth, then the tooth is said to have a rake or hook of 0°. If the face of the tooth leans forward towards this imaginary line, it has positive rake; if it leans backward, negative rake. The greater the rake angle, the more material will be taken out at each pass, but the greater the amount of tear-out on the underside of the timber. With a lower rake angle a smoother cut is ensured, but more pressure will be needed to feed the work into the blade. Blades with negative rake are designed for radial-arm saws and sliding compound mitre saws, or for use in cutting metals. A positive hook of 5 to 15° produces the best results for wood cutting.

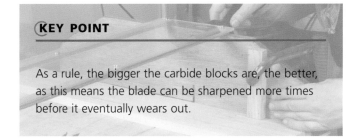

KEY POINT

As a rule, the bigger the carbide blocks are, the better, as this means the blade can be sharpened more times before it eventually wears out.

ABOVE Examples of blades with positive (foreground) and negative rake.

FOCUS ON:

Thin-kerfed blades

This type of blade, which is gaining popularity, has a thinner body and narrower teeth than standard blades. The advantage is that less material is removed during a cut, so feed speeds are quicker and less power is needed. But cutting is not necessarily cleaner, as the thinner blade is more prone to vibration. They also heat up more quickly and expand more easily, so their staying power is reduced.

ABOVE A thin-kerfed blade.

Bevel angle

The other significant factor determining the cutting performance of a saw tooth is the shape of its cutting edge as seen across the thickness of the blade. This may either be ground straight across (flat-top or FT teeth), or bevelled, with each tooth sloping in the opposite direction to the previous one (alternate top-bevel or ATB teeth). The steeper the bevel, the cleaner the cut, but the sooner the teeth will blunt. A 15° bevel is typical, but steeper angles are available, up to 25° on steep top-bevel (STB) teeth.

The flat-top tooth acts like a chisel, peeling the wood fibres away, and works much more effectively with the grain than across it. It is a good choice when speed of cut is more important than a fine finish, so its main use is in ripping down stock to manageable sizes, prior to final dimensioning.

Some blades feature flat-top teeth (known as *rakers*) alternating with other types of tooth to help to clean out the cuttings or chips.

A good-quality 'combination' blade will often feature alternate top-bevel teeth; here a shearing action is employed to cut through the timber, giving a minimum of tear-out when working across the grain. Better finish can be achieved with a steeper bevel angle or with a greater number of teeth, but a 40-tooth ATB is a good all-rounder. Some ATB blades have flat-topped raker teeth also.

A final configuration is the trapezoidal-flat or triple-chip (TC) tooth, where each alternate tooth has both its corners chamfered to 45°, the remaining teeth being either flat-topped or alternate-bevelled, each acting to clean up the cut of the preceding tooth.

ABOVE In this ATB combination blade, intermittent flat-top teeth clear out the kerf as it progresses.

Some workers prefer this type when working with man-made materials, plastics or non-ferrous stock. They can be used on solid wood, but are not as effective as ATB blades.

Gullets

These are the spaces or pockets between the teeth, which carry out the waste from the cut. The deeper the gullet, the more waste can be taken out, but their size is invariably more than ample for most tasks.

Expansion slots

The friction of the cutting process generates a great deal of heat, so most good blades feature laser-cut expansion slots which allow the metal to expand slightly without distorting. The number may range from two or three evenly spaced around the perimeter of the blade, to elaborate slot designs covering the whole of the blade body.

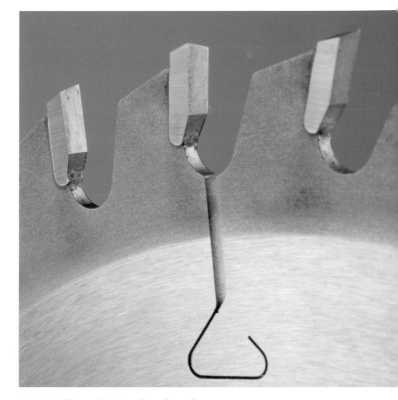

ABOVE Alternative top-bevel teeth.

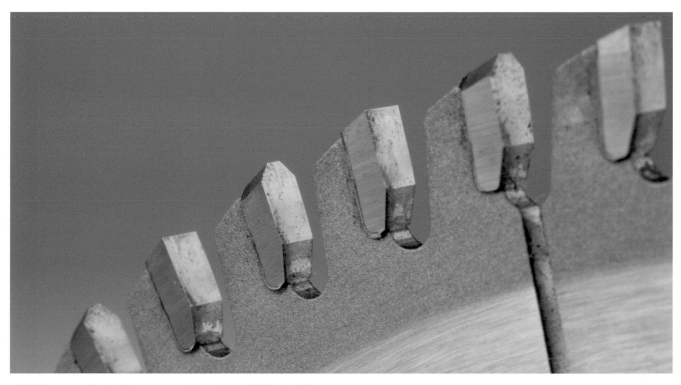

ABOVE Triple-chip teeth; an expansion slot is visible at right.

Choosing a blade

For most sawing operations involving solid wood, it is perfectly possible to get by with only one blade. It has to be of suitable quality to cope with crosscutting as well as ripping: well designed, with at least 40 sizable TCT teeth of ATB configuration. If this is your preferred route, make sure you choose a sturdy blade with a reputation for long life and high-quality performance. Take some advice and do some research. A top-quality blade may cost two or three times as much as a mid-market model. The brazing on the teeth will be smooth, finely ground and without any pitting. There will be a number of expansion slots, a precisely engineered arbor hole which fits the spindle perfectly, and the body of the blade will be very flat.

But it may be a better option, and even an economy in the long run, to have a selection of blades:

- a ripping blade of about 24 teeth, coarse enough to handle any thickness of stock within the limits of the blade diameter
- a crosscut blade of at least 40 teeth for general cut-off work
- a fine-cutting blade with in excess of 60 teeth for finishing to length.

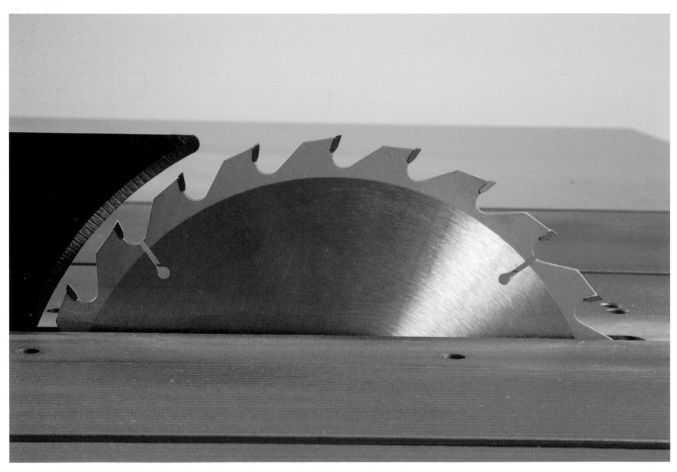

ABOVE A 24-tooth blade for rough cutting.

ABOVE For high-quality finishing this blade has 100 teeth.

For sheet material and laminates, a triple-chip blade would be the best choice to avoid tear-out or chipping, and this would also be suitable for plastics and non-ferrous metals. Blades of this type are long-lasting, given that the density of materials such as MDF can quickly dull a sharp edge. But a decent 40–60-tooth ATB blade should also give a clean finish on these materials.

KEY POINT

When buying a new blade, ensure that it complies with the standards in force in your country or state. In the UK, the relevant standard is BS EN 847-1: 1997.

Common blade types

The vital statistics of a tablesaw blade are:

- blade diameter
- arbor hole diameter
- width of the tooth
- pitch or hook angle (see page 77)
- bevel angle (see pages 78–9)

The first three of these are determined by the size and design of your saw, so you will need to check the saw manufacturer's instructions before choosing which blade to buy.

1 Ripping blade
A dependable, robust blade for ripsawing both hard- and softwoods, and occasional rough crosscutting. For use where finish is of least importance.
Pitch: 20°
Bevel angle: 10°

2 General-purpose blade
A combination blade giving a good finish for both ripping and crosscutting operations. For use on hard- and softwoods, man-made boards, etc.
Pitch: 10°
Bevel angle: 10°

3 Fine crosscut blade
For smooth crosscutting, sizing, trimming, mitre cutting on timber, plywood, particle boards, soft plastics, etc. Gives a clean finishing cut.
Pitch: 10°
Bevel angle: 10°

4 Finishing blade
For fine trimming and finishing applications in double-sided laminate boards, veneers and hard plastics. Eliminates finishing in many operations.
Pitch: 10°
Bevel angle: 10°

5 Triple-chip blade
An extra-fine-toothed blade with triple-chip tooth form. Suitable for clean cutting of plastic sheets, laminates, veneered and melamine-faced boards.
Pitch: 10°
Bevel angle: alternate teeth are chamfered at 45° on both corners; remaining teeth are flat-topped and 0.008in (0.2mm) shorter

6 Non-ferrous blade
For cutting thin-walled extrusions of aluminium and other non-ferrous metals, including bronze, copper, brass, zinc, etc. Also suitable for plastic extrusions.
Pitch: –5° (negative rake)
Bevel angle: alternate teeth are chamfered at 45° on both corners; remaining teeth are flat-topped and 0.008in (0.2mm) shorter

7 Negative crosscut blade
For cutting across the grain and trimming in radial-arm, pendulum and pull-over saws.
Pitch: –5°
Bevel angle: 10°

8 Narrow-kerf blade
For extra-fine trimming of thin extrusions in plastic and aluminium. To avoid blade damage, special attention should be paid to work-holding and feed rate.
Pitch: –15°
Bevel angle: alternate teeth are chamfered at 45° on both corners; remaining teeth are flat-topped and 0.008in (0.2mm) shorter

Special-purpose blades

Scoring blade

This is a small blade which runs in the opposite direction to the main blade and reduces the risk of tear-out by scoring a shallow cut in the workpiece prior to the main cut. The blade measures about 4in (100mm) and is a feature of some panel saws engaged in heavy-duty production, often with sheet materials, rather than standard site or cabinet saws. That said, it is possible to retro-fit a scoring blade to a cabinet saw.

Dado blade

More common in the US than Europe, this consists of a single, wide blade or a pair of bevel-toothed blades separated by flat-topped 'chippers'. It is intended for grooving or rebating – that is, for cuts which do not pass all the way through the timber. A single dado blade will normally take out two or three times as much stock as a standard saw blade; a stacked dado head will allow a much greater width of groove, though there are safety issues (see panel opposite) due to the amount of material removed. If using this method, it is essential to fit an appropriate blade guard, such as those described on pages 38–9, and to use this in conjunction with push sticks, hold-downs and featherboards. The table insert will need to be customized or replaced to accommodate the width of the stack, and a zero-tolerance insert is advisable, to provide full support for the material as it passes through.

However, many European saws nowadays employ a shortened arbor which precludes the use of a stacked dado head, and EU health and safety rules (PUWAR) recommend that cuts such as grooving or rebating should be carried out with more suitable machines, such as a vertical spindle moulder or a router.

ABOVE A scoring blade set in advance of the main blade.

Moulding head

The same caveats apply to the moulding and grooving block, which consists of a circular steel block with two housings or recesses holding a pair of specially shaped cutting blades. Trenching, rebating, tonguing and grooving cuts are all possible.

Again, this is a potentially dangerous piece of tooling which removes a large amount of waste material with one pass, and European saws are likely to be designed so a moulding head cannot be used. Safety guidelines stress that this kind of operation can be carried out more safely and more effectively with a dedicated spindle moulder, or on a router table.

FOCUS ON:

Dado heads and user safety

Safety regulations in the European Union strongly discourage the use of stacked dado blades, especially those over ⅝in (16mm) wide. The making of tablesaws with long arbors which permit the use of dado blades is also discouraged, though at least one imported US model has this feature. The blade brake which is required to be fitted to tablesaws in the EU could cause dado blades to break loose, with disastrous consequences.

Cut all your grooves and housings (dadoes in US usage) the safe way, with a router and straightedge.

Changing the blade

ABOVE A locking pin locates in a dedicated hole in the arbor through the table to hold it firm while a spanner (wrench) loosens the arbor flange.

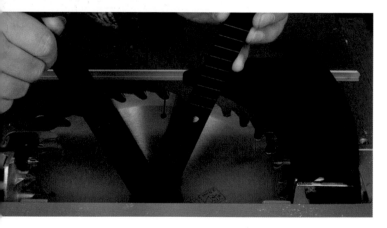

ABOVE Use two spanners: one to hold the arbor in place, the other to undo the arbor nut.

This simple operation will need to be carried out on a regular basis. The blade will need to be maintained properly as a matter of routine, and this is done far more effectively if it is removed from the spindle.

To change the blade:

1 First make sure the tablesaw is disconnected from the power source.

2 Remove the table insert (throat plate).

3 Lock the arbor in place with the wrench or locking pin provided.

4 Loosen and remove the arbor nut with the wrench provided.

5 Check the blade and clean, sharpen or replace as necessary.

6 Remove any dirt from the arbor, arbor flange nuts and threads.

7 Lightly oil the blade.

8 Replace the blade, making sure it sits squarely and firmly in position.

9 Replace the arbor nut, and tighten firmly but do not overtighten.

Blade care and maintenance

High-quality saw blades cost quite a lot, so take good care of them by using the correct blade for the job and maintaining it regularly. It takes no time at all for deposits from the woodcutting process to build up in the gullets and on the teeth of a saw blade. Should you ignore this, there will be a dulling effect on the blade, increased friction and heat, increased vibration, and a risk of warping or even cracking the blade.

Some woods – pine for instance – contain more natural resin than others; this pitch, if not removed, will harden and carry on building up over time, impeding accuracy when cutting. Water-soluble blade-cleaning solvents are environmentally sound and do the job well enough, but you can also keep the blade clean by immersing it in a tray or bucket with a little petrol (gasoline) or paint remover and scrubbing with a stiff toothbrush, wire brush or similar. Used plastic pizza trays are fine for this. Do make sure your hands are well protected.

When you have finished, check the teeth carefully for any chipping, which can if necessary be repaired by a saw doctor. Make sure that the blade is completely dry before returning it to its arbor; you can dry it manually, but it is quicker and safer to use a water-repelling spray such as WD40.

Resharpening a carbide-toothed blade needs to be carried out on a precision grinding machine; doing it by hand is not an option, so make sure that whoever takes on the task is properly equipped to do so.

ABOVE If the blade needs a lot of cleaning, use wire wool in the first instance.

KEY POINT

Though carbide tips on teeth are tough, resilient and long-lasting if maintained properly, they are also rather brittle, so care must be taken when handling and storing them. Never stack TCT blades directly on top of one another or place them on ferrous surfaces, and never use them on timber which may contain nails or screws.

ABOVE AND RIGHT Keep saw blades packaged properly when not in use. Do not stack them on top of each other.

BLADE CARE CHECKLIST

- Tungsten carbide is an extremely hard but brittle material that needs to be handled with care. Never let the teeth come into contact with any metallic or hard surface, such as another blade. Even a slight tap on a metal surface, such as the saw table, can chip or crack a tooth.
- Store in a cardboard folder or wooden box when not in use, and treat with rust-preventative oil.
- Keep the blade clean and free from sticky deposits of resin, etc.

- Always ensure the blade is revolving at full speed before starting to cut.
- Ensure blades are kept sharp at all times. TCT blades stay sharp for long periods, but must be sharpened as soon as they become dull. Continuing to use a dull blade is a false economy: it causes faster wear on the tooth edge, which means more carbide needs to be removed during resharpening.

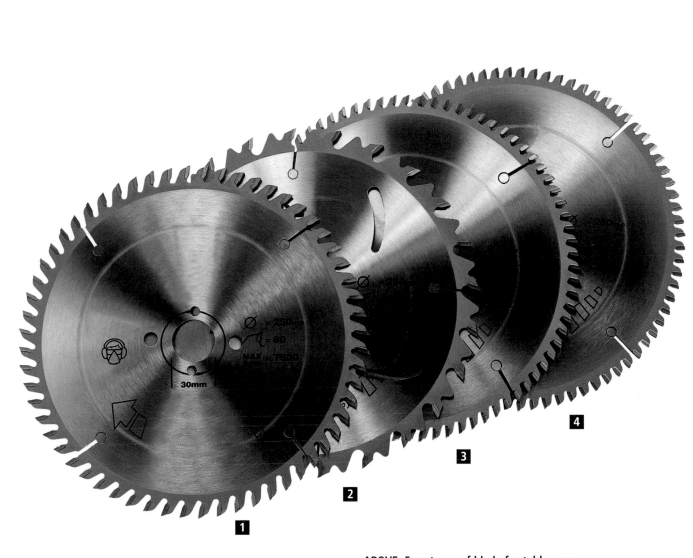

ABOVE Four types of blade for tablesaws:
1: ATB crosscutting blade
2: ripping blade with anti-kickback teeth
3: triple-chip blade with positive rake
4: triple-chip blade with negative rake.

Part 2:
Basic Techniques

2:1 Working safely

According to statistics provided by the Health and Safety Executive in the UK, in a recent study of 1000 accidents involving woodworking machines, 35% occurred on the tablesaw; most of these resulted in the loss of fingers. The great majority of incidents occurred while the operator was ripping or crosscutting, with the blade guard either removed or incorrectly adjusted. These accidents could easily have been avoided had the guard been properly in place and a push stick used, as in the photograph opposite.

I make this point, not to frighten you off using the tablesaw, but to remind you that the regulations and recommendations regarding machine use are there for your protection. Read this section thoroughly, familiarize yourself with the regulations in force in your country or state, and follow these recommendations at all times – never be tempted to cut corners.

Legal requirements

Each country or state has its own safety regulations, and you should obtain a copy of those which apply in the area where you live. In the UK, for example, the requirements relating to circular saw benches are covered in the Provision and Use of Work Equipment Regulations, 1998 (PUWER 98), and supported by the Approved Code of Practice (ACOP), Safe Use of Woodworking Machinery, 1998. All of these recommendations are recognizable in a court of law; this means that if you flout the advice and an accident occurs, you may well be considered culpable and have no redress in law.

Training and instruction is a central requirement of PUWER 98. Hand-fed circular saws should not be operated by any person under the age of 18 unless they have undergone an approved course of training. A younger person will need supervision by a suitably qualified operator with a thorough knowledge and experience of the machine and its safeguarding requirements.

ⓕFOCUS ON:

Prohibited uses

Under PUWER 98, the use of a circular saw for the cutting of any rebate, tenon or groove is prohibited, unless the part of the blade above the table is effectively guarded. When it is not practicable to carry out these operations with the riving knife and top guard in position, suitable alternative guards and fixtures are necessary.

The use of a circular saw for 'stopped grooving' cuts, which end before passing fully through the timber, is not recommended. This operation can be carried out much more effectively on a spindle moulder or with a router.

ⓚKEY POINT

Should you buy a new circular saw bench in the UK, it must come with a declaration of conformity and have a CE mark. The design and construction of the machine must comply with BS EN 1870-1: 1999.

RIGHT The CE mark is a declaration of conformity for new machines in the European market.

Always use push sticks

Use push sticks to keep your hands away from the blade. Take some time to prepare a selection of sticks for various types of work. They are easily run up from scrap timber, and easily replaced when damaged. Get into the habit of using them at all times. Health and safety guidelines in the UK state that a push stick must be used when making any cut less than 12in (300mm) in length, or when feeding the last 12in of a longer cut. Use a more substantial push block when deep-cutting timber to produce thin offcuts.

When making a cut, the leading hand should never be closer than necessary to the front of the saw, and hands should never be in line with the saw blade. As soon as my leading hand reaches the front edge of the table I switch to a push stick.

When removing the wood between the blade and the fence after a pass, again a push stick should be used, unless the width of the wood exceeds 6in (150mm), in which case it is deemed safe enough to remove it by hand.

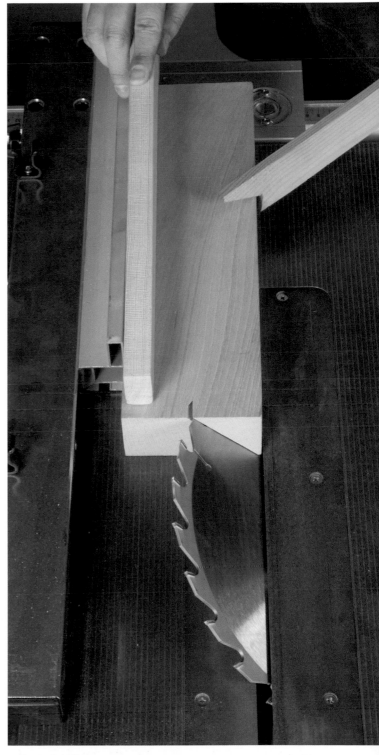

ABOVE A selection of home-made push sticks for various cutting tasks.

ABOVE Push sticks are easily made up, so there is no need to be precious about them. Use two if necessary.

Workpiece support

An essential factor in all operations at the tablesaw is the provision of adequate support for the work. If you are handling large workpieces, use extension tables, at both the infeed and outfeed sides of the main table if necessary.

If you choose to use an extra pair of hands to collect the work as it passes through the saw blade, then the outfeed table should be extended so the distance between the saw blade spindle and the back of the table is at least 4ft (1200mm), and your assistant should remain at the outfeed side of the table without reaching forward towards the saw. The riving knife will reduce the risk of contact with the blade, but will not necessarily prevent it.

Ripping, crosscutting and angled cuts all require the aid of fences or jigs sturdy enough to support the work safely and effectively. If shallow or bevelled work is to be carried out, then very occasionally the standard fence may need to be replaced by a low fence in order to aid the use of the push stick or to prevent a canted saw blade touching the fence. This low fence need be nothing more than a strip of stable timber, perhaps 2in (50mm) square, clamped to the rip fence or directly to the table. Occasionally the rip fence on a tablesaw is adjustable and can itself be canted, instead of angling the blade, as shown on page 119.

Timber with a round cross-section must be clamped to a moving fence or to a specially designed jig; if this proves difficult, it may be more suitable to cut the timber on a bandsaw.

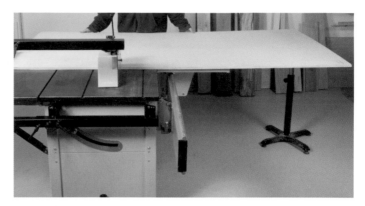

ABOVE This wide board requires both a side extension table and a side support.

BELOW An assistant can be useful when handling long boards, but must stand well away from the blade.

Fingerboards and hold-downs

By holding the workpiece firmly against the fence and table, these devices play an important part in the prevention of kickback, whilst allowing the operator to keep both hands safely away from the saw blade. They are in a sense secondary to the first line of defence – the riving knife and the blade guard – but they are essential in situations where one or both of these cannot be used.

Hold-down units and fingerboards (featherboards) come in an array of shapes and sizes, and can also be home-made to suit your saw with a little thought and creativity.

A fingerboard can be made up in no time from a length of scrap timber approximately 10 x 4in (250 x 100mm) with reasonably straight grain. Make a diagonal cut of around 60° across the face at one end, and from that end make a series of cuts for a distance of about 4–6in (100–150mm) along the length of the board, parallel to its long edge. Now you have a featherboard which can be clamped to the table top, tight against the work, to hold it firmly against the rip fence.

Kickback remains the major safety problem for tablesaw users, but the safety devices discussed here will greatly reduce the danger, provided they are used intelligently and consistently.

ABOVE Using a hold-down to support a wide board.

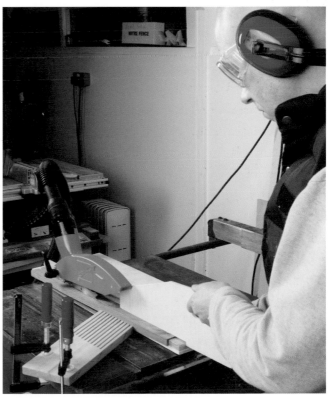

ABOVE A home-made fingerboard supporting the workpiece against the rip fence.

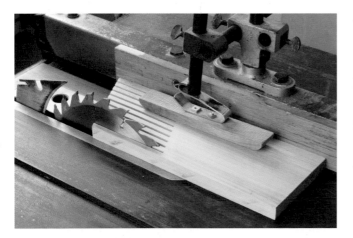

ABOVE A hold-down being used in the making of a fingerboard.

Brakes

Blade braking systems make for safer woodcutting, especially on machines where the work is hand-fed. In the UK, they have been compulsory since 2003, with certain exceptions. They are not considered necessary on machines which have a run-down time of 10 seconds or less – which is the case with many of the newer tablesaws on the market – or on those built in conformity with a harmonized European Standard which does not require a braking system.

One common problem with the tablesaw, as with other workshop machinery, is that the operator may either forget or be unaware that a blade is still running; and because there is a stroboscopic effect of light on a revolving blade, it can appear to be stationary while still in motion. Never put your hand near the blade, or attempt to adjust the blade guard or riving knife, until you are quite certain that the blade is stationary.

FOCUS ON:

Automatic braking

One American range of tablesaws – available only in the US at the time of writing – features a sensor device which is able to detect the electrical conductivity of the skin if it contacts the saw blade. On detection of this foreign matter – a human finger, for example – a brake is applied; the blade will come to an abrupt halt, within one quarter of a turn, and then retract swiftly below the table, leaving the operator with a minor cut as opposed to an amputated finger. Should the sensor detect metal, the same process will kick into action to protect the blade from damage.

Unfortunately, the sensor cannot be retrofitted to existing machines, as its implementation calls for an internal redesign of the tablesaw. It remains to be seen whether it will become a standard feature.

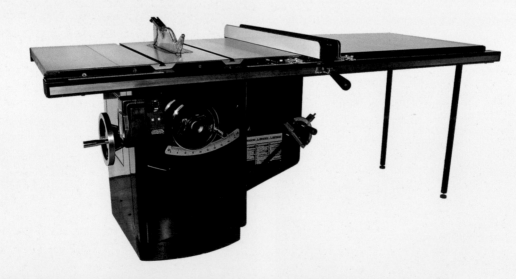

ABOVE The braking system of this American tablesaw is a recent contribution to workshop safety.

Noise

Noise levels will vary from one machine to another, and depending on the conditions of use. If you are exposed to high noise levels for even a short time, you may experience temporary partial hearing loss. Continued exposure may lead to permanent hearing damage, which can be severe.

In the UK, the Woodworking Machines Regulations require employers to take reasonable practicable measures to reduce noise levels if employees are likely to experience constant noise of 90 decibels (dB(A)) or more over an 8-hour working day. In addition to this, suitable ear protection must be provided, maintained and worn. If you are working on your own account, you owe it to yourself to be aware of the damage to hearing that can easily be caused by continuously high noise levels.

Use ear defenders as a matter of course. If you find standard earmuffs cumbersome (they can interfere with safety spectacles or goggles), try the extremely lightweight hearing bands which are much less intrusive in use.

ABOVE Ear defenders and safety glasses: essential items for every tablesaw user.

Eye protection

Use of the tablesaw can result in large amounts of airborne material in an enclosed space, and eye irritation or injury is very likely unless sensible precautions are taken. Always take dust seriously – do not regard it as merely part and parcel of the nature of the work. Choose eye protection which is comfortable, given that the spectacles or goggles may have to be worn for long periods at a time, and try to use a pair which will neither fog nor scratch. Some are antistatic, some claim to be impact-resistant, others are tinted. More usefully, some wrap fully around the eyes for greater protection.

FOCUS ON:

Eye injuries

- In most cases, washing thoroughly with cool, clean water will suffice; use an eyecup if possible so as to keep grubby fingers away from the eye. A small piece of sterile gauze can be used to gently wipe the eyeball if necessary.
- If this does not solve the problem, use a sterile ring bandage or similar to keep the eye protected and free from pressure, and seek medical attention immediately.
- Never attempt to remove the offending article with tweezers or any other hard object.

As always in health and safety matters, prevention is better than cure. Goggles may be inconvenient at times, but they are much less inconvenient than the damage which may be caused by not wearing them. Don't take chances with your eyesight.

Dust control

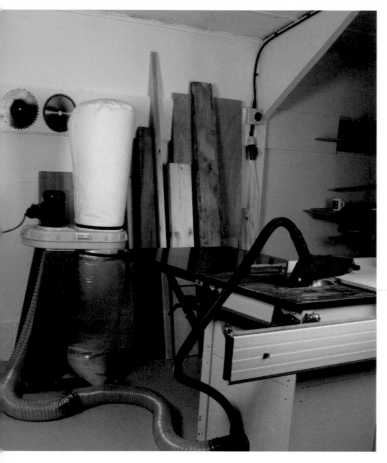

ABOVE Extraction from above and below the table.

ABOVE The large amounts of wood dust made by the tablesaw must be contained as effectively as possible.

Unless managed efficiently, dust is a major problem for woodworkers, whether on site or in the workshop. The tablesaw will throw out a great deal of it. It is harmful to both eyes and lungs, and also carries a risk of fire or even explosion. Exposure to any kind of dust is hazardous, but some types of wood dust are worse than others, causing differing levels of skin, eye or breathing irritation, allergic reaction, asthma, and even cancer of the nose or throat. The dust created by composite materials such as MDF, certain plywoods, and other laminates is equally harmful. The dust will spew out as high-velocity flying chips at one end of the scale, down to micro-dust particles at the other. The latter are far more dangerous: these are the particles which cause respiratory problems by getting deep into the lung tissues, unless preventative action is taken.

A circular saw bench should be fitted with extraction both above and below the table. A well-maintained and airtight under-bench hood will complement any extraction system, making good use of the air movement caused by the rotating blade. Sometimes, though, conflicting air flows from the extraction system and the work may cause air turbulence and increased noise levels. In such cases, internal guide

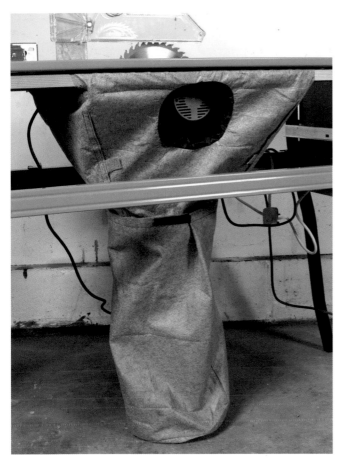

ABOVE **This model comes with efficient under-table extraction.**

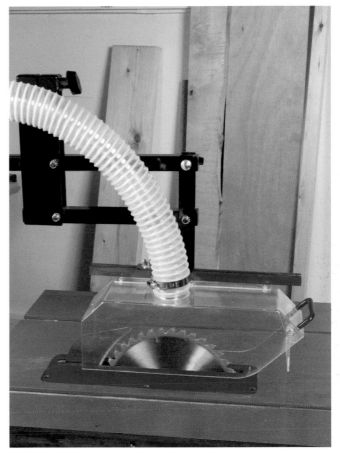

ABOVE **Extraction above the blade guard.**

vanes can be used in order to optimize airflow rates and reduce noise. These can be fitted by the user if not supplied with the saw.

A range of face masks is available. The moulded sort, which fits round your nose and mouth and has a breather valve, is among the most practical. Masks are classified according to the type of dust they protect against, and the degree of protection is printed on the packaging to facilitate selection. A very effective but expensive way of protecting eyes and lungs simultaneously is with a full-face battery-powered respirator. In these, a stream of filtered air is

blown down over the face and out at the bottom of the mask. They are excellent for spectacle wearers because they keep your lenses clear, unlike some other types of goggles.

KEY POINT

Efficient dust extraction, combined with the use of a dust mask, safety glasses, ear defenders, adequate blade guarding and a sharp saw blade will minimize the many risks associated with wood dust, making your working environment a great deal safer and more pleasant to operate in.

Saw-blade safety

- The riving knife (splitter) must be matched to the blade being used. It should be rigid and set accurately in line with the blade as described on page 60. It should be shaped so that the inner edge follows as closely as practicable the contours of the largest blade that can be used on your particular machine.

ABOVE A correctly fitted riving knife closely follows the shape of the blade.

ABOVE The blade guard rests on the workpiece as it passes through the blade.

- The blade guard should be strong, with a flange at either side, and adjusted as close as possible to the surface of the workpiece.

- Make sure you have the right blade for the job in hand. Choose a good combination blade to cover most of the bases, or a blade specific to the task, such as a ripping or crosscut blade as appropriate.

- Always select the correct diameter blade specified for your machine. Use of the wrong size will affect the peripheral speed and thus the cutting efficiency. Select the best pitch for the material being cut: at least one tooth should always be in contact with the material to control the feed rate.

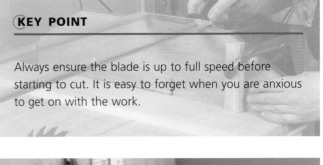

KEY POINT

Always ensure the blade is up to full speed before starting to cut. It is easy to forget when you are anxious to get on with the work.

ABOVE Setting the blade height.

ABOVE On the right-hand label the blade diameter ('Blattdurchmesser' in German) is stated as 200mm (8in) minimum, 270mm (10¾in) maximum.

Small pitches (more teeth) are essential for thin materials, whilst larger pitches (fewer teeth) are suitable for thicker material.

- Set the blade height correctly. Though it is a debatable point, I find that having about a tenth of the saw blade projecting through the workpiece during a cut is fine. This can be judged accurately enough by eye. When cutting thin materials this should be reduced so that the blade is barely projecting through.

- The feed rate should be smooth and continuous. Dwelling in the cut will tend to dull the teeth and may cause burn marks; go too quickly, and you run the risk of slowing or stopping the blade.

- Ensure blades are kept sharp at all times. Keep the blade clean and free from sticky deposits of resin, etc. Dull, badly set and badly ground blades will require extra effort when feeding the work through, and this in turn increases the risk of accidents.

KEY POINT

Never try to clean a running blade; make sure the machine is completely stopped, then remove the blade and clean it properly. Remember that a moving blade can sometimes appear to be stationary.

ABOVE This blade is turning at speed but appears static.

General workshop safety

- Loose clothing can be dangerous, especially patch pockets and wide sleeves, which can snag on guards, fences, etc. The smocks favoured by woodturners are very practical, with their tight cuffs and pockets at the back. Always wear steel-capped shoes in the workshop. Long hair should be tied back or restrained under a hat. Any loose items such as jewellery should be removed.

- Maintain a safe electrical supply. Circuits must be adequate for your power requirements and in good condition; plugs (preferably rubber, for durability) must have correctly rated fuses. Do not overload the sockets with multi-socket adapters; a multi-way extension lead is neater. Label each plug to show which one is for which tool; this will ensure that you unplug the correct tool before adjusting it or changing cutters. If your main power box does not already have circuit breakers instead of ordinary fuses, residual-current circuit-breakers (RCBs) will protect you against a fault in the wiring. If starting from scratch, try to arrange for the power box to be located by the door so that you can break the main switch as you go out, if necessary. Exterior power cables must be armoured. Get professional advice and installation if in any doubt whatsoever.

- Overcrowded and untidy workshops increase the risk of accidents. Make sure there is a clear path to the exit at all times: you might want to leave in a hurry one day.

- Do not let large quantities of shavings and dust accumulate; they present a fire hazard, and can also be slippery. Rubber non-slip matting provides a much better surface to stand on.

- A fire extinguisher suitable for electrical fires – *not* a water extinguisher – is essential. Put it where it can be easily reached, preferably by the exit. Learn how to use it and make sure you have it checked at the specified intervals.

When working with machinery of any kind, you should keep a well-stocked first aid box readily available, with relevant emergency telephone numbers easily accessible. A minimum kit is listed on the next page.

ABOVE Keep your workshop fire extinguisher in a visible, easily accessed location.

ⓕ FIRST-AID KIT

- Antiseptic ointment
- Antiseptic spray
- Antiseptic wipes
- Good-quality sharp tweezers (not to be used on or near the eyes)
- Scissors
- Plasters (wound dressings)

- Butterfly plasters
- Adhesive tape
- Sterile pads of various sizes
- Cold compress
- Eyewash
- Mild painkillers
- Sterile gloves

Remember to replace items as and when they are used.

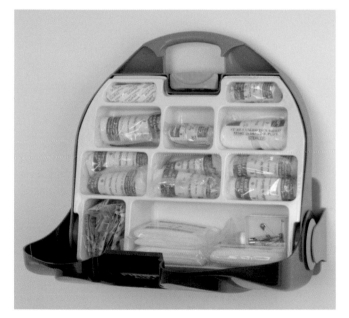

ABOVE Your first-aid box should be in a prominent location and easy to find in an emergency.

RIGHT An emergency eyewash station is also worth having.

2:2 Ripping

Cutting a piece of timber along its length – with the grain – is known as ripping.
To reduce the width of the workpiece to the required dimension it is slid along the rip
fence of the tablesaw, which has first been set to the appropriate distance from the
blade. The edge of the wood which is butted up to the fence must be prepared straight
and flat beforehand so that it lies fully flush with the fence. Ripping is really the primary
function of a tablesaw, and the operation at which it excels.

ABOVE Starting to feed the timber into the saw.

Basic principles

For good results you must always:

- select the right blade for the job
- set the height of the blade correctly
- adjust the fence to the required setting
- make sure all safety features are in place and you are wearing appropriate protective clothing
- and only then proceed to make the cut.

Making sure you are safe and comfortable, with nothing to hamper cutting, feed the work through the saw blade at an even, steady rate: neither too slow – or burn marks may show on the timber – nor too quickly, which would tax the motor. A little experience will rapidly bolster confidence, and you will learn to listen to the saw to judge whether the feed speed is right.

Stance

First make sure all the table-top features are aligned correctly – blade, riving knife, guard and fences – and that the surrounding area is free from anything which might obstruct the cutting process. Have the necessary hold-downs and other safety aids in place; it is especially important to have the correct push stick (see page 93), which will allow you to move the workpiece fully through the blade without getting your hands near the teeth. Position yourself comfortably at the front of the saw, with safety glasses and ear defenders on, before switching on the machine. Stand as close to the table as is comfortable, so you are not in any danger of over-reaching. Then, supporting the work at the rear with one hand whilst keeping it firmly against the rip fence with the other, begin the cut. The leading hand should stay well away from the moving blade, which should be properly guarded and revolving at full speed before the work passes through it.

ABOVE A comfortable stance, with the leading hand well away from the blade. A long piece of timber can safely be fed in by hand at first, but a push stick will be needed for the last 12in (300mm) or so. This picture shows the SUVA guard in use (see page 39).

⊙TECHNIQUE:

As you move in towards the tablesaw, place your leading foot against the base of the saw and your hip against the front rail – this will give you support and stability during the cut.

Working with irregular timber

Not all of the stock you work with will be straight and true – it is possible that some preparation will be needed in order to get the timber into the correct condition for effective ripsawing. This may mean planing up a straight edge or a flat face, which can be done either on a dedicated planing machine or with a hand plane. Work to a marked line, and if there is much waste to be removed, saw off as much waste as possible before planing. Thicknessing – planing both faces of the timber – may also need to be carried out in order to achieve fully parallel surfaces.

Another method of straightening out uneven sides is to attach a straight-edged board which overhangs the edge of the workpiece, giving a true surface from which to work. You can then run the guiding edge along the rip fence as you rip the workpiece on the opposing side, giving a straight edge which can serve as the basis for the rest of your cuts. If the straight board is attached using small nails or brads, the face of the timber can be cleaned up easily afterwards.

Alternatively, you can quickly make up a jig or a sled, such as the simple example shown opposite.

Perhaps the simplest method of dealing with uneven-sided timber is by using the saw's sliding table, if you are lucky enough to have this facility. It is found on many European-type tablesaws.

ABOVE The sliding table on this European-style saw is a useful ally when dealing with irregular stock.

(FOCUS ON:

The ripping sled

This simple device merely consists of a baseboard made of MDF or close-grained ply, with a runner on its underside which fits snugly into the mitre-gauge slot in the table top. It slides smoothly along the table with the timber resting securely on the baseboard, which allows an accurate cut to be made even when the wood does not have a straight surface to ride against the rip fence. Some slightly protruding brads or countersunk screws driven into the baseboard from below (just visible in the photographs) will help to keep the work in place.

ABOVE This view shows the guide runner (arrowed) which fits into the mitre slot on the table top.

ABOVE A simple sled for achieving a straight edge.

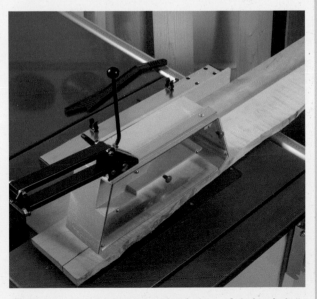

ABOVE An uneven or waney-edged piece of timber being cut straight.

Working with defective timber

It is occasionally necessary to rip a piece of timber which has not been prepared fully, and whose surfaces are not flat. Various approaches can be used, depending on the nature of the distortion.

Cupped boards

A piece of wood is said to be 'cupped' when shrinkage has pulled its sides together in an elliptical fashion, so that it is curved from side to side, though it may be straight along its length. Attempting to flatten the face before ripping may result in a lot of wastage – better if possible to reduce the cup by ripping the wood into narrower pieces before flattening the face.

Care must be taken when ripping a board which has cupped. The safest method is to secure the timber to a sled – or to the sliding table if you have one – with the hollow side downwards for stability. Take particular care as the blade comes to the end of its cut: at this point the two sawn pieces will collapse downwards, with the possibility of kickback. A thin wedge inserted between work and table should help with this, and the riving knife and guard should also give adequate protection.

Laying the timber the other way up, with the convex side resting on the table, can be dangerous: it may rock slightly, again giving rise to the possibility of kickback. With very irregular boards the use of a stopped auxiliary rip fence or half-fence (see page 43) is essential.

If you do not have the use of a sled or a sliding table, it may be safer to cut the wood on a bandsaw.

ABOVE A home-made half-fence provides extra stability.

Bowed boards

Boards which are curved along their length are best cut on a bandsaw; however, it is possible to carry this operation out safely on a tablesaw. Keeping the hollow face on top, the leading edge of the work can be pressed flat to the table and guided through the blade with a suitable push stick, so the front of the timber is always flat to the table; the other end can be supported by placing a wedge underneath. A small hold-down clamped to the rip fence, sitting just above the work and placed just in front of the blade, may assist the operation.

Twisted boards

This would be a dangerous operation to carry out on the tablesaw, given the difficulty in maintaining solid contact between the timber, the table and the fence.

It may be possible to reduce the twist by crosscutting the workpiece into shorter lengths, giving some workable stock.

Crooked boards

A board which is curved in its plan view will not ride securely against the fence. As with twisted wood, it is better to use a bandsaw. However, if you fix the work to a ripping sled a clean edge can be achieved.

Knots

Always keep an eye out for knots – dimensioning wood to its final size and then finding a knot or two near the edge can be infuriating. Some knots you can work with, and they can even be a 'feature', but only if they are sound. If you are unsure, knock them out and plug the holes later, or work around them.

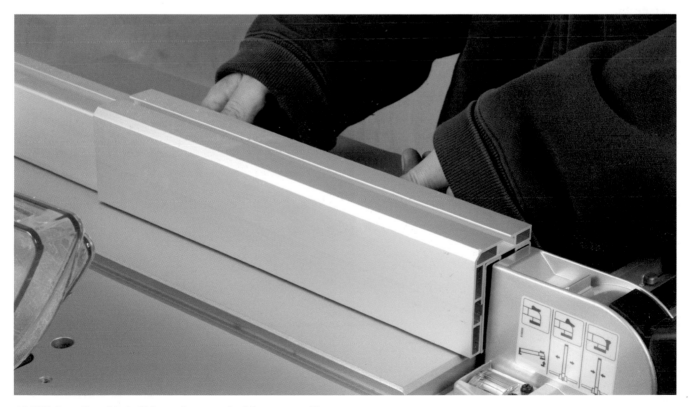

ABOVE An adjustable half-fence is a standard feature on this saw.

Ripping long boards

Ripping boards of any length over 3ft (1m) is made easier by the addition of an outfeed table at the same height or just a little lower than the main table. One may already be fitted to the saw, or be available as an accessory; or you may have to make your own, which can be anything from a simple, portable stand or 'horse' to a more elaborate, possibly even permanent fixture. Roller stands can be useful additions to any workshop – easily portable, sturdy and safe to use. They can, however, occasionally guide the work in an undesirable direction if they are not set in the correct position behind the table, and this may take the cut off line or even jam the work up against the blade.

Another method of coping with lengthy stock is to enlist the aid of a willing helper – hopefully someone who is familiar with the workings of the saw – who will gently but firmly support the work from beneath as it comes off the table, without pulling or resisting it as it passes through the blade. Your assistant should stand a little way back from the end of the saw – more than arm's length, if necessary – out of the danger zone.

Passing very long boards through the blade can be a tricky operation: it is critical that the work lies flat to the table and square to the fence on its journey, so it must not be allowed to sag. On occasion I use extra support on the infeed side to take the weight of the board as I feed it through the saw. I find this a safer option than standing at a distance from the saw and trying to control the workpiece from there.

As when cutting wide stock on the tablesaw, stance is important. Use one hand to keep the wood tight up against the rip fence for the duration of the cut, while the other hand feeds the work through.

ABOVE Outfeed support is supplied here by an extending arm.

ABOVE Using an extra pair of hands for outfeed support.

KEY POINT

As a matter of course, when ending a cut on a long piece of timber, always use a push stick to move the work fully through the saw blade.

LEFT It can be difficult to control the path of the work if you are too far away from the table. Infeed support allows you to stand closer, giving more control when handling longer stock.

ABOVE Controlling the wood with the left hand while the right hand steadily feeds the work through.

Ripping narrower stock

ABOVE One push stick (at top) feeds the wood forward, while another keeps it close against the rip fence.

A few problems will arise when trying to rip down narrow boards, unless precautionary measures are taken. Because the rip fence is so close to the blade and guard, there is little room to use a push stick. By making up a long, narrow push stick, and using a second one to steady the workpiece, this problem can be overcome.

It is possible to make the cuts on the opposite side of the work – that is, so the finished workpiece is on the side of the blade furthest away from the fence – but this would entail readjustment of the fence after each cut, which is not really satisfactory.

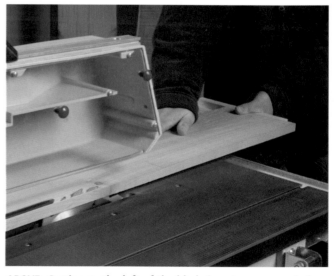

ABOVE Cutting to the left of the blade is not recommended for repetitive cuts.

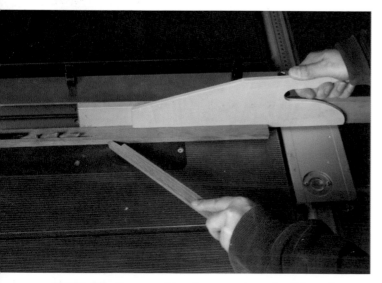

ABOVE Effective use of two home-made push sticks to keep narrow stock safely under control.

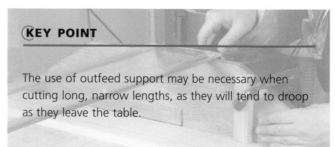

KEY POINT

The use of outfeed support may be necessary when cutting long, narrow lengths, as they will tend to droop as they leave the table.

ABOVE This simple jig gives more room between blade and fence to accommodate a slimline push stick.

Alternatively, by clamping a straight strip of material between the rip fence and the blade, set at the required distance for the narrow stock, more room is made available to operate the push stick, making the whole process much easier and safer.

Another simple solution is to make up a quick jig with a stop notched out of the side and a handle for manoeuvring; the whole ensemble rides the rip fence when set to the correct distances.

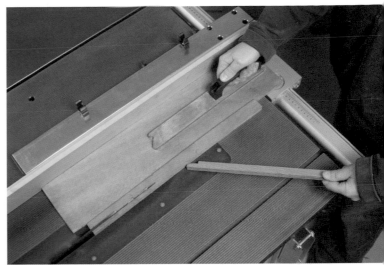

ABOVE A handy jig for ripping narrow stock, shown without the blade guard for clarity.

ABOVE The handle of the jig seen in close-up.

KEY POINT

If you have made up a zero-tolerance throat plate (see page 59), this will come in useful here, as really narrow strips can easily slip through the gap between blade and table insert, sometimes resulting in violent kickback.

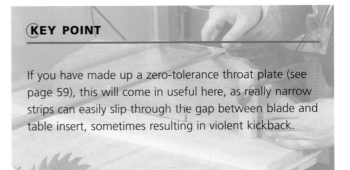

Ripping wide or sheet materials

If your main area of work is carpentry, do-it-yourself or even certain branches of furniture making, you may often have cause to cut down large 8 by 4ft (2440 x 1220mm) boards. This can be something of a challenge due to their general unwieldiness, weight, flexibility and overall size. Good support, to the rear of the table and to the side, is the key to managing this situation – unless you have a helper at hand. Without adequate support, waste material will fall to both the side and rear as the work passes through the blade, causing the material to ride up and skew dangerously between the blade and fence. This could easily result in injury to both operator and machine.

> **⊙TECHNIQUE:**
>
> You may want to cut down the sheet into manageable portions, either by hand or with a circular saw, prior to dimensioning on the tablesaw. There is no need to make life difficult for yourself by struggling with large pieces of material if you can avoid it.

The good news is that as there is no grain structure as such in sheet material, there is no risk of kickback resulting from natural timber movement.

ABOVE Cutting a wide board with the aid of side support and a sliding table.

ABOVE Sheet material can be cut without any additional support, but extension tables make the job much easier.

As when ripping long pieces of timber, your stance in relation to the saw and the workpiece is important, and additional workpiece support is a great help. The operation can at first can seem daunting, but with a little experience it gets easier. Once the board has been manoeuvred onto the table and the power switched on, slightly raise the corner of the material opposite to that which is passing through the blade. Looking towards that opposing corner, move forward steadily as the work moves through the blade, always maintaining enough pressure to keep the work firmly against the rip fence. Finally, as you close in to the table, move directly behind the material, in line with the cut, to complete the movement as normal.

When the cut is complete and the waste material has fallen onto the outfeed or extension tables, turn off the power, then collect up the work and the waste.

KEY POINT

Because sheet material does not distort, you can use a full-length rip fence without any danger of pinching the blade as it passes through.

FOCUS ON:

Reducing tear-out

With some sheet materials, tear-out can be a nuisance, especially if you have expensive, good-quality veneered surfaces to cut. To reduce the amount of tear-out there are several options:

- Use the correct blade (see page 82).
- Make sure it is clean and sharp.
- Check that the surface which will be seen is uppermost on the saw table.
- Use a zero-tolerance table insert.
- Score an initial cut prior to the secondary main cut, if you have a suitable scoring blade (see page 83).
- Keep the blade high.
- Stick masking tape over the line of the cut before you begin to saw.

Ripping bevels

ABOVE The blade set for a bevelled cut.

ABOVE Avoid this scenario, where the fence is tilted towards the blade and the work can easily become trapped.

Once the blade-tilt wheel had been adjusted to the desired angle, the operation is really no different from a standard rip cut: you simply move the workpiece along the rip fence and through the blade, using push sticks as usual. However, the rip fence will have to be moved appropriately, depending on which side the blade is tilted: if it tilts to the left, the rip fence should sit to the right of the blade, and vice versa. Allowing the blade to tilt towards the fence is potentially dangerous, as the work moving through the cut may become trapped between the two, causing kickback.

SAFETY

Use a blade guard when you can, and use push sticks for the last 12in (300mm) or so of any cut. Note that the perspective in some of the photographs makes the hands look closer to the blade than they really are.

ABOVE Ripping with the blade tilted away from the fence is much safer. The blade guard has been removed for clarity.

BELOW A tilting rip fence giving a bevelled cut or chamfer.

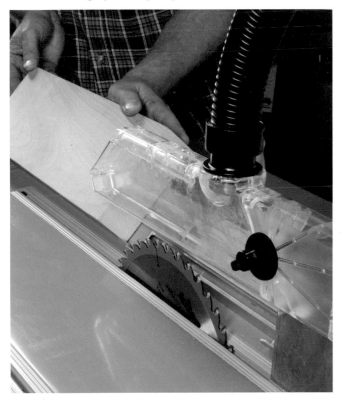

ABOVE Another acceptable method, using push sticks and with a shortened auxiliary rip fence to avoid kickback. The blade guard has been removed for clarity.

Another way of performing bevelled cuts is with the aid of a tilting rip fence, allowing the blade to remain at 90° to the table – though this is not a standard feature on many tablesaws.

Lastly, creating a simple 45° jig is a quick and easy way to replicate the most commonly used angled cut. This is described on pages 164–5.

Angled cuts or tapers

This is another operation which calls for a jig. Whether a basic, simple affair or a more elaborate design, this is a most useful addition around the workshop for tapering such items as table legs or wedges. For details, see page 163.

ABOVE A tapering jig cutting a slender table leg.

Resawing

This operation is certainly not recommended for the tablesaw, though many woodworkers do it simply because it allows the cutting of stock which is thicker than the blade's maximum depth of cut. The process involves making the first pass with the blade set at just over half of the depth of the work, then flipping over the wood so the same face rests against the rip fence and making a second pass to cut the wood in two.

This is an operation best carried out on the bandsaw, but with the use of a crown guard and push sticks it is possible to use the tablesaw. However, on the first pass the blade is buried completely in the workpiece and the waste material has little by way of an escape route, which means that the blade can heat up and bind, making for a potentially dangerous situation. Do not use this method if you can avoid it.

KEY POINT

Remember that non-through cuts, such as the first cut in the resawing process, cannot be made with a standard blade guard in place. They must therefore not be attempted unless your machine is fitted with a crown guard or other appropriate safety device (see pages 38–9).

ABOVE Making the first pass when resawing.

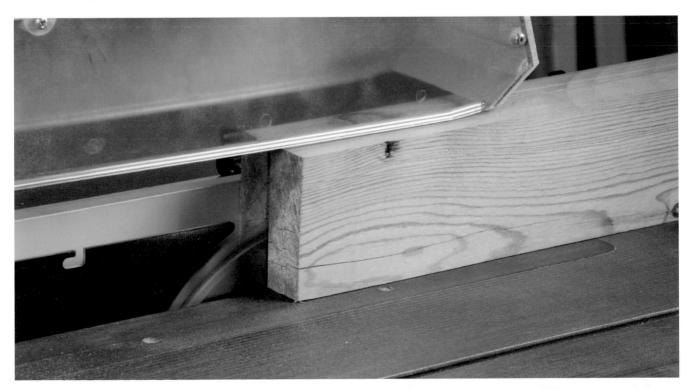

ABOVE The workpiece flipped over for the second pass. It is much better to use a bandsaw for this operation.

Basic principles

Because you are actually cutting through the grain fibres, the kerf will not pull together as occurs with ripping, so there is much less chance of the work binding on the blade and being thrown back at you. Added to this, because the work is invariably guided by a fence or jig rather than being fed through independently by hand, the whole cutting process is less dangerous than ripping. The wood can also be readily clamped to the mitre fence before cutting, which makes accurate work easily achievable.

The mitre gauge itself is merely a protractor head, which should sit at 90° to the saw blade and which rotates through 60° to either side, giving a wide range of cutting angles. The gauge is retained by a single guide bar which sits in the mitre slots milled into the table top at either side of the blade. Crosscutting accuracy and control can be greatly improved with the addition of an auxiliary fence to the mitre gauge, or by the use of a dedicated jig for each operation, as described in Part 3.

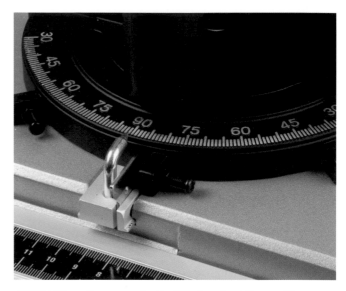

ABOVE The mitre gauge by itself is too short for working longer lengths of stock.

ABOVE A mitre fence with a hold-down to clamp the work down, and a drop-down stop for accurate and repeatable crosscutting.

(FOCUS ON:

The mitre gauge

At the outset it is vitally important to ensure that the mitre gauge is set up correctly, as described on pages 64–5. It must be at exactly 90° to the saw blade, with the dedicated stops set to the correct positions on the gauge, and the face of the fence must be perpendicular to the table. The guide bar must fit firmly into the mitre slots with no room for give.

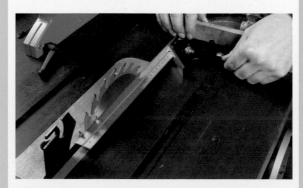

ABOVE Checking the adjustment of the mitre gauge in relation to the blade.

Cutting to length

Square off one end of the workpiece first, then square the opposite end to the correct length. With the aid of a stop clamped to the mitre fence or jig, accurate repetitive crosscutting to length is simple enough to achieve. Some mitre fences come with this facility in place; if yours did not, it is easy enough just to clamp a small block to the face of the fence to serve as a stop.

Another way of cutting a series of short pieces to a uniform length is to clamp a small stop block to the rip fence; but this must stop short of the front edge of the saw blade so the work cannot bind between the stop and the blade. The end of the wood is butted against this stop, and the work is then moved forward in the usual way, using the mitre fence to keep it square.

ABOVE A stop block clamped to the rip fence; it is positioned well in front of the blade to prevent binding and kickback.

ABOVE This mitre fence has an auxiliary stop for repetitive crosscutting to a consistent length.

(KEY POINT

Always have a push stick at the ready for when you have completed the crosscutting operation. Use it to move the offcut away into safety so it cannot catch on the spinning blade and be thrown out towards you.

Some useful accessories

Basic auxiliary mitre fence

This useful addition to the standard mitre fence improves control over the workpiece, giving a lengthier, more stable base to guide the wood. This feature comes as standard with many tablesaws, but if yours does not have one, just make your own. Use a length of straight-grained hardwood, no less than 1in (25mm) thick, and affix it to the existing slots or holes in the mitre gauge. Make it slightly overlong at first, so you can use the tablesaw itself to cut the fence to size, thus giving a reference point for further cutting. Leave a small gap of about ⅗in (5mm) between the base of the new fence and the table top, or make a rebate of this size in the face side of the fence; this gap or recess will serve to combat the build-up of wood dust which can hamper accurate cutting.

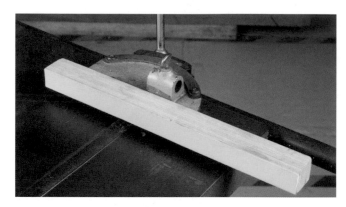

ABOVE An additional fence fixed to the standard mitre fence.

KEY POINT

It is a good idea to fit some fine abrasive paper to the face of the fence which will help to grip the workpiece; this gives a rougher surface to hold on to when cutting.

ABOVE An auxiliary mitre fence comes as standard on many tablesaws.

Superior auxiliary mitre fence

With a slightly more elaborate design it is possible to add functionality to a home-made mitre fence. The model shown here includes a sliding scale and a measuring stop. Again it is fixed to the existing mitre gauge, reaching from the blade to the outer limit of the saw table.

The L-shaped stop is held in place simply by an inverted bolt and oversized plastic gripping nut. The head of the bolt is housed within a sliding dovetail on top of the mitre fence, machined out with a router and dovetailing bit.

A clear plastic marker is fitted to the top surface of the stop, with an inscribed centre line which indexes against the scale fitted to the top of the fence. Both scale and marking gauge can be purchased from wood, power-tool, craft or hobby retailers.

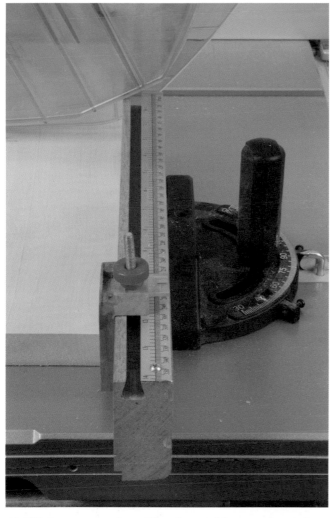

ABOVE A custom-made auxiliary fence with measuring scale and stop. A small rebate allows for dust build-up.

ABOVE A close-up of the stop and marking gauge.

ABOVE The improved mitre fence in use.

Sliding table

A sliding table is a luxury that not every woodworker can boast of. However, if you are lucky enough to have this facility on your machine it does allow for safe, quick and easy crosscutting of both solid timber and sheet material.

Especially useful when crosscutting large, heavy and unwieldy pieces are those tables which are integral to the tablesaw; these will give accurate results with little effort. Add-on sliding supports require more care, but a well-designed sliding support system is certainly a welcome workmate capable of easing the difficult task cutting larger material.

ABOVE A sliding table with its own mitre fence.

ABOVE Long and heavy lengths of timber are cut easily using a sliding table.

⊙KEY POINT

Keep the rip fence well away from the blade and the workpiece when crosscutting.

ABOVE Do not push the work through the blade using the offcut side – one hand should be on the mitre gauge and the other on the work side.

ABOVE A well-designed sliding support system.

ABOVE The system differs from an integral sliding carriage, but can still support quite substantial pieces of work.

A valuable addition to the whole sliding table system is an adjustable mitre fence, so that work can be angled as necessary.

ABOVE The sliding carriage with mitre fence can be used for angled work.

Blades for crosscutting

This subject has been discussed more fully in Chapter 1:4, but it is worth repeating that with the advent of highly efficient tungsten-carbide-tipped blades, a good-quality finish can be obtained in both ripping and crosscutting with the same general-purpose blade. It will need to have at least 40 teeth,

but 60 or even 80 would work well. The configuration of the teeth should be alternate-top-bevel or ATB (explained on page 78), to help reduce tear-out when cutting across the grain. The angle of the bevel will affect the cut: the steeper the bevel, the better the finish, but the more quickly the teeth will blunt.

Crosscutting jig

A recommended method of crosscutting without the use of a mitre gauge is to make or buy a jig designed specifically for the purpose. The principal benefit of this is the confidence of knowing your crosscuts will be square, time after time, without the constant checking and readjustment needed when using a mitre fence.

As with many other tablesaw jigs, the one shown here consists of a solid base with two runners which slide in the saw table's mitre slots. More detailed information will be found on pages 140–9, but suffice to say that a well-constructed jig should be a great time-saver, and make the job a deal easier too.

ABOVE A simple but well-made crosscutting jig.

Crosscutting techniques

ABOVE The correct approach: the left hand, holding the workpiece, is well away from the blade; the right hand is safely behind the work, using the locking lever as a handle.

With the blade set to the correct height, place your workpiece firmly against the face of the mitre fence or jig, so that it lies flat on the saw table or the baseboard of the jig. Line up the cut in relation to the saw blade, taking care to work to the waste side of the line marked out on your workpiece. Should your auxiliary fence extend right up to the blade, you can use the end of the fence as a cutting guide. For added security, the work can also be clamped to the mitre fence.

Stand to the same side of the blade as the mitre fence, and allow the blade to reach maximum speed. Then, with one hand holding the workpiece against the fence (if it is not clamped in place) and the other moving the gauge and the work through the blade, complete your crosscut. Start slowly, easing the saw teeth into the work, and speed up gradually as the cut progresses.

The offcut is easily removed if it is 10in (250mm) long or more – simply move it to the side, away from the blade, either by hand or with a push stick as appropriate. Very small offcuts may fall away of their own accord; but they may also become trapped between the table insert and the blade, in which case the saw must be shut down and the offending article removed before beginning again.

For repeated cutting, as previously mentioned, it is perhaps best and certainly easiest to use a drop stop if your mitre fence has one; otherwise, clamp a stop block to either the mitre fence, the rip fence or the crosscut sled.

ABOVE Safe crosscutting on a portable saw.

(F)FOCUS ON:

Holding the work safely

Do not hold the offcut side of the workpiece to guide it through the cut. This is a dangerous practice, as your hand will be directly behind the moving blade. You may also inadvertently move the offcut into the blade, causing kickback.

Make sure the offcut does not become trapped between rip fence and blade, or simply get tangled up with the running blade – in either case it may be thrown back at you.

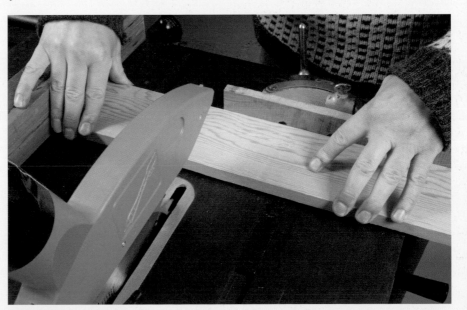

ABOVE How not to do it: the rip fence here is too close to the workpiece and could cause a dangerous kickback. Moreover, the right hand will be passing behind the blade, which is asking for trouble.

Crosscutting sheet material

ABOVE The mitre fence is to the front of the workpiece, which is securely clamped down.

This is best carried out on a sliding carriage, or at least with the aid of some side supports; rear supports may also be needed. As when ripping wide material, unless the work is supported all the way through the cut and beyond into safe removal space, then dangers are at hand. A standard mitre gauge will be of no use for wide panels, though an auxiliary mitre fence may be adequate. Place the fence to the front of the workpiece, clamping down if possible, and feed the work through the blade.

If using a crosscutting jig or sled – which is a good alternative for crosscutting long boards – it is simple enough to clamp a stop block to the front of the sled to hold down the workpiece, which might otherwise ride up due to uneven weight distribution.

ABOVE A simple hold-down will clamp the workpiece in place.

ABOVE This short piece on a crosscutting jig is being held down manually, using an offcut at least 10in (250mm) long.

Crosscutting short pieces

It is essential to keep fingers well away from the blade, so when cutting short pieces – a practice not ideally suited to the tablesaw – some form of hold-down must always be used for safe and stable cutting. A standard mitre gauge alone does not give adequate support, but with an extended auxiliary fence the work can be carried out safely, and the same technique can be used on a crosscutting sled. An oversized auxiliary fence, 4in (100mm) or more in height, provides useful extra support and kickback protection – but it must end below the height of the blade guard.

ABOVE Crosscutting short stock using an oversized auxiliary mitre fence. A saw cut in the fence itself makes a useful guide when lining up the work.

Cutting mitres

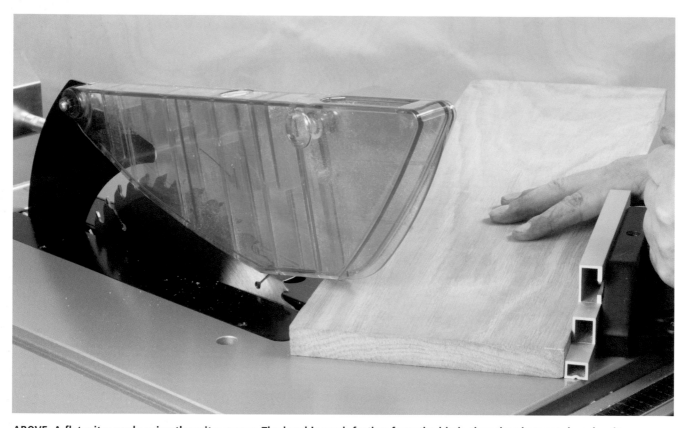

ABOVE A flat mitre made using the mitre gauge. The hand is much further from the blade than the photograph makes it appear.

A flat mitre – in which the workpiece lies flat on the table, with the blade perpendicular, and is angled in plan view only – can be carried out with the aid of the mitre gauge set to the required angle. The mitre fence can either be positioned behind the workpiece and used to push it through the cut, or placed to the front of the work and used as a guide for pushing it through the blade. Whichever you choose, if the mitre fence face has abrasive paper affixed to it there will be much less risk of unwanted movement. Attaching stops to the mitre fence will also help stabilize the operation, as well as allowing repeated cuts to be made to the same dimensions. This is particularly useful for mitre cutting, as paired pieces are often needed – for example, to make the opposing sides of a frame.

Because the most common angle cut on the mitre gauge is 45°, a jig dedicated to that angle can save much time when setting the gauge. Simple to construct from a block of stable, straight-grained timber, it features two grooves, one on each face, which sit securely on the mitre bar of the gauge. (The two grooves cannot be exactly back to back, but must be offset to avoid weakening the jig too much.) With the end cut to a perfect 45° angle, aligning the gauge to the jig gives a correct angle every time.

A dedicated jig for making mitring easy works on the same principle as a crosscutting jig. It is a great time-saver and guarantees perfect 45° mitres time and again. Its construction is described on page 162.

It is a good idea to make a stop for a mitre fence from an offcut sawn to 45° – the most common mitre angle. This can be clamped to the fence supporting the workpiece, without damaging the corner.

ABOVE A home-made stop attached with clamps.

ABOVE A simple jig to verify a 45° angle on the mitre gauge.

ABOVE This dedicated 45° mitring jig is easily made, as described on page 162.

Bevels or end mitres

Should the saw blade be set at an angle to the vertical other than 90°, this is termed a bevelled mitre. The procedure for this is the same as for other crosscutting operations, except that the blade is tilted to the desired angle. This cut is often needed in picture framing or for joining mouldings in joinery (interior trim), and is sometimes known as an end mitre. Again, using the dedicated jig shown on pages 164–5 this operation can be greatly simplified.

Compound mitres

A combination of flat mitre and bevelled cut is known as a compound mitre. In this case the blade is tilted to the required angle and the workpiece is pushed through it by an angled mitre gauge, using the same techniques as previously discussed.

ABOVE A compound mitre in progress, using the mitre fence in conjunction with a tilted blade.

ABOVE The finished compound mitre.

ABOVE A 45° bevelling jig.

FOCUS ON:

Crosscutting safety

When you are crosscutting, make sure that the rip fence is well away from the work being sawn. Do not use the rip fence as a stop block for repeated cuts, unless you are using the arrangement shown on page 125, with an additional block to prevent kickback.

The purposely staged photograph below shows some of the things you must *not* do:

1 Hands are wrongly placed behind the blade, risking serious injury.

2 The blade guard and riving knife are not in place.

3 The rip fence is tight against the work, in danger of binding against the blade.

4 Push sticks are too far away to be reached easily.

5 Loose clothing could be caught in the blade.

6 The operator is using no eye or ear protection.

7 The saw table is dangerously cluttered.

8 Wiring is draped over the mitre fence.

At least this operator has taken pains to ensure that his hair cannot be trapped in the blade.

ABOVE An accident waiting to happen. Never get yourself into this situation.

Part 3:
Making and using jigs

3:1 Crosscut sled

If set up correctly, this particularly useful jig will give consistently accurate results, as well as improved safety for the user, since it gives much greater purchase and stability to the workpiece. It should to a great extent replace the mitre fence as your primary means of crosscutting. Its only shortcoming is that the blade cannot be tilted to make bevelled cuts, for which an alternative method will have to be found – either a dedicated jig, or the standard mitre gauge. The principle is simple enough: a sturdy, flat base which moves across the table by means of two guide runners which fit firmly but freely into the mitre slots milled into the top of the saw table. Accuracy here is the key to a successful jig.

The saw must be set up correctly for the sled to work: the blade must be set parallel to the mitre slots, and the fence of the jig must be perpendicular to both.

Construction

Cut the two runners from a suitable hardwood – I used mahogany – and, using a sharp chisel, gradually scrape the sides until they fit perfectly in the mitre slots. They should be tight, but not too tight to move; once they are fixed to the base they can be waxed for free running. Metal or plastic runners would be equally suitable.

ABOVE Squaring an edge using the crosscutting sled.

The base, which must sit flush to the table, should be made from stable, close-grained ply or MDF which will move smoothly across the table – birch ply is good. It need not be too thick, or much of the blade's cutting height will be lost; ½in (12mm) is adequate. The base should overhang 1in (25mm) on either side, while finishing flush with the table front and back. The overhanging sides allow for the placing of a stop to halt the run of the sled as the blade finishes its cut.

ABOVE Guide runners in place, with a coat of wax for reduced friction and smooth running.

(FOCUS ON:

Jigs

A jig is an aid designed to improve the efficiency of a specific task, resulting in more effective and safer production. The best jigs tend to be reasonably simple and straightforward to construct, but all should be sturdy and accurately made, so as to produce equally accurate work. It is generally best to make a dedicated jig for each task, rather than trying to create an all-purpose problem-solver.

Most tablesaw jigs make use of the rip fence or the mitre slots in the table top as guide rails. The workpiece must be held securely, and the user must be effectively guarded from the saw blade at all times. This is an important point, because some jigs cannot be used in conjunction with a standard blade guard, so alternative guarding will need to be provided (see pages 168–9 for examples).

In addition to the jigs described in Part 3, you will undoubtedly need to make some of the simple safety accessories described in earlier chapters:

- push sticks (see page 93)
- fingerboards or featherboards (page 95)
- zero-tolerance insert (page 59).

ABOVE The stop will connect with the clamp to halt the travel of the sled at the appropriate point.

3:1   Crosscut sled

ABOVE The blade passes through a slot in the rear fence...

**ABOVE ...into a wooden exit guard which also gives added
support to the fence.**

With the base clamped squarely to the table top, mark out the positions of the mitre slots. This will allow you to locate the guide runners on the base, which can then be fixed carefully in place with screws and glue.

Front and rear fences are made from ply, at least ¾in (19mm) thick – laminating a couple of sheets together is a good idea – and at least double the height of the blade when fully extended. The fences are secured to the front and rear of the base with countersunk screws and strong wood glue. Make sure the screws are not in the path of the saw cut, or in the way of any modifications you might wish to add to the jig. The back fence sits along the back edge of the base, while the front fence is set 3in (75mm) in from the front edge to allow for full blade travel. A small rebate at the base of the front fence will allow for dust build-up and chip clearance.

The front fence must be absolutely perpendicular to the base and exactly square to the blade; this is critical. It may take some manoeuvring to achieve this, but by screwing one end of the fence firmly to the base and slightly elongating the countersunk drill hole in the opposite end, small adjustments can be made. With the aid of an engineer's square, a true working surface will be obtained.

 An auxiliary block guard needs to be fitted, functioning as a run-out port for the blade and giving extra support to the fence. When fixing this guard, again be wary of where the path of the saw cut will be so as to avoid placing any fixing screws in the way. I have supplemented this safety aid with an additional handle; this is not strictly necessary, but removes the temptation to push the sled using the

ABOVE The handle fitted to the exit guard keeps hands well away from the blade.

exit guard – although the hands would naturally grip the front fence at a safe distance from the blade in any case.

Test for accuracy by cutting a piece of timber, flipping it and butting up the two pieces as you have done before. If it is not quite right, adjust by elongating the screw holes as before. When satisfied, add strong glue, clamp if possible and, when set, drive in some extra screws.

Blade cover

The blade must be properly guarded during the cutting process, so a safe and secure cover will need to be designed for your jig. I chose a simple design, using a length of clear acrylic plastic, supported by two strips of hardwood and fixed to the top of the front and rear fences. It will shield the user from debris thrown up from the blade, and keep hands away from the teeth, although when the sled is used correctly the hands are naturally placed well away from the blade.

KEY POINT

It is important to keep the riving knife in place when using a crosscutting jig. Lower it to slightly below the top of the blade to permit rebated and grooved cuts. These cuts are best made with the aid of hold-downs.

ABOVE Crosscutting with the aid of a hold-down; note the positions of the hands during this operation.

3:1   Crosscut sled

Box joints

This is a refinement of the crosscut sled previously described. I use this version to make box joints (also known as a comb or finger joints), which are strong joints often used for assembling drawers or box sides; they have a pleasing look as well as mechanical strength and a large gluing area. It also

ABOVE The sliding plate in situ, with a T-bar for holding work perpendicular to the blade.

> ### KEY POINT
>
> If you want to add extra features to a basic design such as the crosscut sled, careful planning at the design stage is essential. Draw out your design on paper, working out the specific functions of each part, then produce a scale drawing, showing how components will work together and where all fixings will be located. Don't forget to allow for any necessary modification to the blade guard when making any jig which requires direct access over the blade.

serves for kerfing – making a series of parallel saw cuts to enable the wood to bend into a smooth curved shape – as described on pages 148–9. The basis for both operations is an adjustable locating key with which to make cuts or slots of the same width at equal distances apart.

Construction

The indexing mechanism for box jointing on my crosscutting jig is simply a sliding plate with a protruding locating finger or key on the blade side. The locating key is either integral – cut from the hardwod block used for the plate – or an addition – in this case a flat-headed bolt countersunk into the back of the plate. A separately made key is less likely to break than a cross-grained one cut from the solid.

The plate itself is recessed into a stopped groove on the back of the front fence, into which a slot has also been cut. A flat-headed bolt fixed to the plate protrudes through the slot and can be locked off by tightening a wing nut at the front of the fence. This apparatus slides smoothly with the aid of a little wax.

ABOVE Two versions of the adjustable indexing plate and finger for box-jointing.

ABOVE Front view, showing the locking mechanism.

3:1   Crosscut sled

Modifying the blade guard

Some simple changes are needed to give the guard
ensemble forward and backward movement. The
process involves routing out two parallel slots in the
acrylic guard, which are bolted to a pair of small 90°
steel brackets; these in turn are fixed to the rear
fence of the crosscutting jig. When the bolts are loose
the guard, supported by the brackets, can be pushed
back to accommodate the work which is held or
clamped to the front fence. The bolts are then
tightened and work commences.

ABOVE The modifications to the blade guard.

(KEY POINT

Once set up, it is a good idea to do a trial run on some
scrap pieces before embarking on the real article;
remember that any initial mistake, no matter how small,
will be compounded as you move across the board.

Using the jig

Because of health and safety regulations governing
the use of stacked dado-head saw blades in Europe –
and the fact that many European saws have short
arbors preventing their use – cutting a wide slot in a
single pass is not always possible. The locating key
on this jig is therefore made the same width as the
saw blade, and each opening is cut with multiple
passes. The first opening must be the right width and
correctly located if all the others are to follow suit.

The blade must be set just a fraction higher than the
thickness of the workpieces to be joined, so the
fingers stand just proud of the surface after assembly
and can then easily be sanded flush.

ABOVE The blade guard positioned so that it just clears the work.

Mark out the equally spaced fingers on your first workpiece. Start with the work towards the front of the table – that is, on the side of the blade furthest from the rip fence. The first cut is made by butting the workpiece up to the locating pin, which is set back from the blade by the width of one 'finger'; test cuts on scrap wood are recommended. The opening must then be widened to the required width, either by moving the pin slightly for each successive pass or by working freehand. Then move the workpiece over, so that the previously cut segment straddles the pin, and make another series of passes till the pin comes to the end of its travel in the first opening. Repeat until all the fingers have been formed.

When the first workpiece is complete, place the end slot over the pin, then butt up the second, mating piece to it and cut out the first mating recess.

ABOVE Using the T-bar to keep the work perpendicular to the blade, cut out between the fingers at equal intervals, which are determined by the guide pin on the sliding plate. This picture shows the last cut in the sequence.

ABOVE Establishing the first cut on a mating board.

ABOVE The end product: a box joint which now needs only light sanding.

3:1   Crosscut sled

ABOVE Kerf-cutting works particularly well on MDF.

Kerfing

There are several ways to bend a piece of timber or board to make, say, an arch above a doorway or a curved apron around a table. One traditional approach entails building up laminates around a former, gluing up and clamping in place until set. This is quite labour-intensive, and often the wood will spring back some way when the clamps are removed. Alternatively, if you have the facilities or are prepared to construct them, a steam bath can be used to soften up the fibres, thus creating enough flexibility for the wood to be formed into a curve.

A simpler alternative to either of these may be to kerf-bend. Simply by making a series of parallel cuts in close proximity to each other, adequate flexibility can be gained to construct a perfectly smooth curve or bend. The method is quick, easy, gives good results, and requires only a tablesaw. Another bonus

---

(FOCUS ON:

Kerf spacing

There is a geometric method to work out a close approximation of ideal kerf spacing. First determine the desired radius of the curve; then, on a test piece:

1 Make a single cut across the piece.
2 Clamp it to the workbench just in front of the cut.
3 Mark out a distance from that cut equal to the desired radius.
4 Elevate the piece till the kerf closes up.
5 The distance between the radius marking on the base of the workpiece and the workbench top is roughly the distance required between kerfs.

is that the box-jointing jig can be used for this operation without further modification, provided the locating pin of the jig is narrow enough to fit in the saw kerf.

Distances between cuts are slightly arbitrary, but be aware that making them too far apart may not result in the smooth curve required. Added to this, some materials will be more flexible than others. However, keeping the intervals to around ⅝ – ¾in (15–20mm) should work in most cases. Leave at least ⅛in (3mm) between the kerf and the opposite surface. Trying out the cuts on a test piece is the easiest way to judge.

When the cutting is completed, to substantially strengthen the work piece you can spread urea-formaldehyde glue or epoxy resin in the trenches; and should you wish the kerfing to be hidden you can veneer the edges and underside.

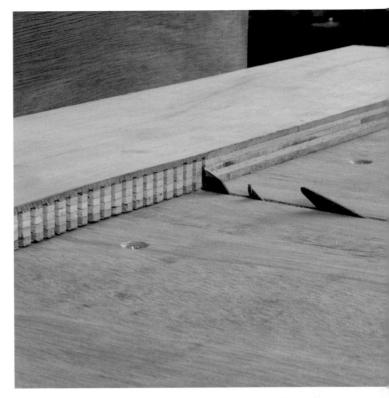

ABOVE Parallel cuts or kerfs ⅝in (15mm) apart on plywood.

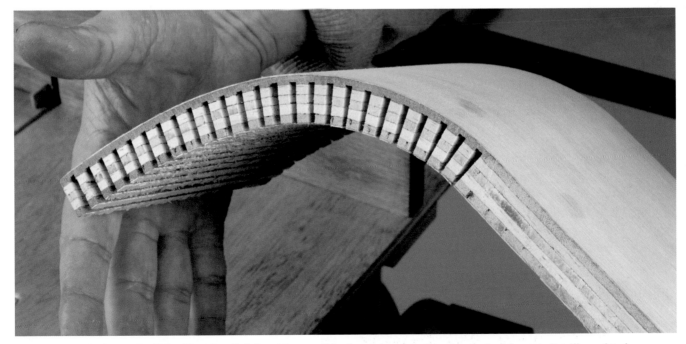

ABOVE Though plywood will kerf-bend well, it is subject to chipping or break-out on the worked face, so it will need to be veneered if that face is to be left visible.

3:2   Tenoning jigs

The mortise and tenon is the most frequently used joint in woodwork. With high mechanical strength, it forms a strong glue joint because of the large long-grain contact area. Mortises can be cut with a chisel mortiser or with a router, but there are no simple solutions to cutting repeated tenons. The following method, adapted with kind permission from articles by Jack Chapman which originally appeared in *The Router* magazine, entails making two separate jigs – one for the shoulders and one for the cheeks – which work together to produce perfect tenons time after time. The jigs may look complex at first sight, but their construction and use are straightforward.

Shoulder-cutting jig

The first jig consists of the following elements:

- A baseboard (A in the drawings), which has a runner on its underside, machined to fit the mitre-guide slot in the saw table.
- A fence (B) which is fixed to the baseboard exactly at right angles to the saw blade.
- A stop (C) which slides along the fence to set the tenon length.
- A clamping piece (E) which slides at right angles to the fence and is adjusted so as to hold the workpiece firmly against it.
- A pair of guards which fully enclose the saw blade. One guard (F), fixed to the baseboard, covers the blade before it enters the workpiece; the other (G), attached to the clamping piece, covers the blade as it exits the cut.

The same jig can also be used to cut a series of workpieces to a consistent length, but for this you will need to make a fence extension with its own sliding stop. The extension fence is screwed to the main fence by means of the holes marked NN in the drawing on page 153.

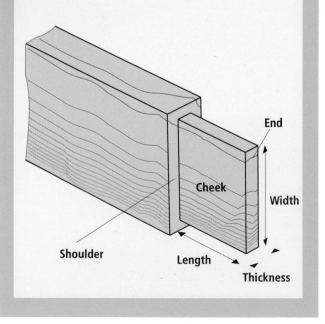

(FOCUS ON:

Tenon terminology

Just to prevent any confusion, here is a summary of the terms used in this chapter to describe the various parts of a tenon.

End

Cheek

Width

Shoulder

Length

Thickness

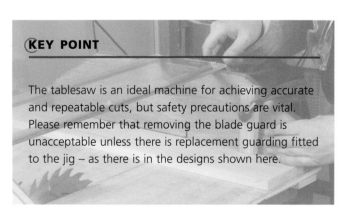

(KEY POINT

The tablesaw is an ideal machine for achieving accurate and repeatable cuts, but safety precautions are vital. Please remember that removing the blade guard is unacceptable unless there is replacement guarding fitted to the jig – as there is in the designs shown here.

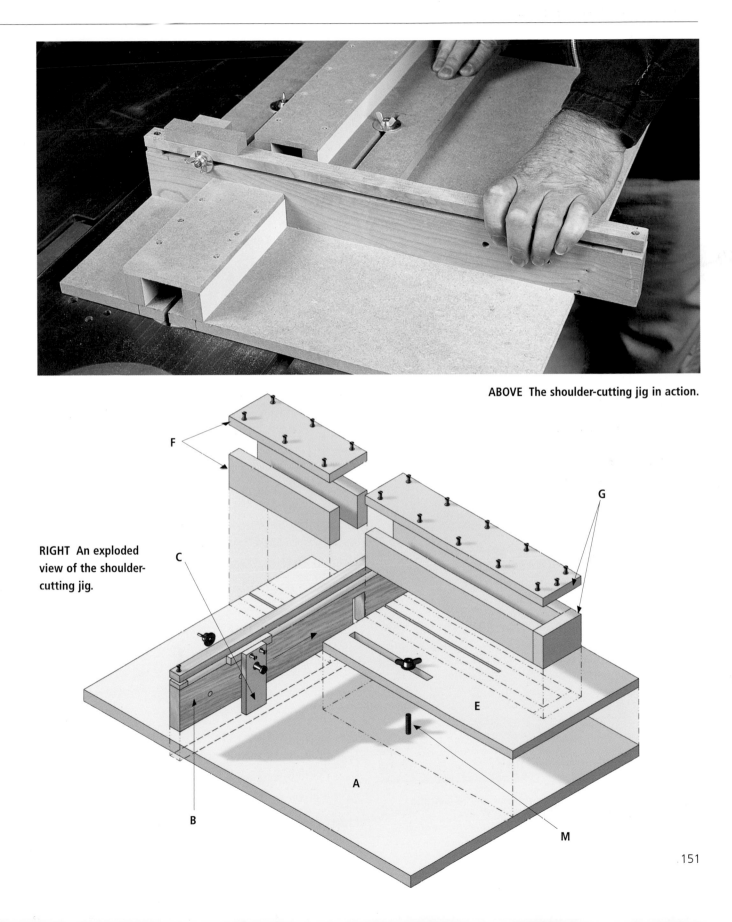

ABOVE The shoulder-cutting jig in action.

RIGHT An exploded view of the shoulder-cutting jig.

3:2   Tenoning jigs

Dimensions

The dimensions shown can be adjusted as necessary to suit your own saw. To determine how long the guards need to be, raise the blade to the maximum height at which it is going to be used – that is, the maximum thickness of the stock to be cut, plus the thickness of the jig baseboard, plus an allowance of ⅛in (3mm) for clearance – and measure the length of blade exposed. In the example shown it was necessary to protect an 8in (200mm) length, so this determined the minimum length of the two guards. Guard F needs to accommodate the full width of the exposed blade, and guard G about half as much again.

The clamping piece E is held by two ¼in (M6) bolts (M) and wing nuts. The distance of these from the fence dictates the maximum width of your stock.

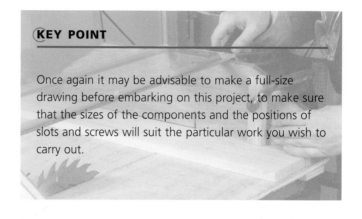

KEY POINT

Once again it may be advisable to make a full-size drawing before embarking on this project, to make sure that the sizes of the components and the positions of slots and screws will suit the particular work you wish to carry out.

If you need to accommodate a greater width of stock, increase the length of the two slots in which these bolts run.

Construction

The example shown is made from ⅝in (16mm) MDF throughout, with the exception of ²⁵⁄₃₂in (20mm) composition board for the guard sides, ²⁵⁄₃₂in (20mm) hardwood for the fence and a hardwood strip for the runner. Hardwood is preferable for the fence, as it gives a better hold for the screws which secure it to the base.

Baseboard and runner

First cut the baseboard to the required dimensions, then make the hardwood runner, which needs to be around 10in (255mm) long. The runner is machined to a close fit in the table slot; one way of doing this is by using a router table and straight cutter. The outfeed fence of the router table is set forward by about the thickness of a sheet of paper. The cutter is then set forward of the infeed fence by the same amount, so you get perfectly consistent, square cuts. Once the fit is good, fix the runner temporarily to the base by countersunk screws at 4in (100mm) intervals, so the blade position is 5in (125mm) from the outer edge of the base. Make sure the runner is square to

ABOVE The underside of the jig, showing the runner that slides in the mitre slot of the saw table.

the leading edge of the base. Position the base on the table and make a 12in (300mm) cut in it; this will be your reference for the fence position. Mark the exact position of the runner, then remove it for now.

The two bolts which secure the clamping piece to the base must be perpendicular. Drill a ³⁄₆₄in (1mm) pilot hole to locate the centre point on both sides of the board, then drill a clearance hole for the bolt head with a Forstner bit, so the head will be countersunk below the board's surface. Finally, drill a clearance hole from the other side to accommodate the thread. The bolts are fixed securely in the baseboard using epoxy resin. Fill over the screw head to make the fixing more secure, and sand the epoxy level when fully cured.

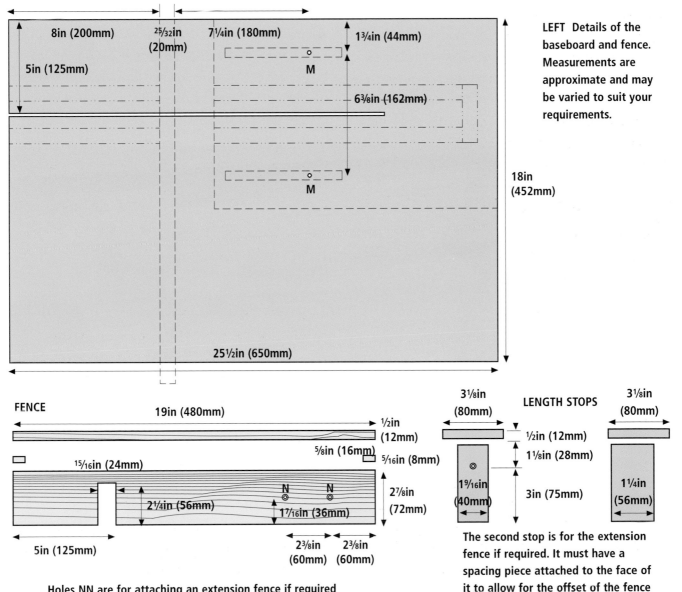

LEFT Details of the baseboard and fence. Measurements are approximate and may be varied to suit your requirements.

8in (200mm)
²⁵⁄₃₂in (20mm)
7¼in (180mm)
1¾in (44mm)
5in (125mm)
M
6³⁄₈in (162mm)
M
18in (452mm)
25½in (650mm)

FENCE
19in (480mm)
½in (12mm)
⁵⁄₈in (16mm)
⁵⁄₁₆in (8mm)
¹⁵⁄₁₆in (24mm)
N   N
2¼in (56mm)
1⁷⁄₁₆in (36mm)
2⁷⁄₈in (72mm)
5in (125mm)
2³⁄₈in (60mm)   2³⁄₈in (60mm)

Holes NN are for attaching an extension fence if required

LENGTH STOPS
3⅛in (80mm)
3⅛in (80mm)
½in (12mm)
1⅛in (28mm)
1⁹⁄₁₆in (40mm)
3in (75mm)
1¼in (56mm)

The second stop is for the extension fence if required. It must have a spacing piece attached to the face of it to allow for the offset of the fence

3:2   Tenoning jigs

Fence and stop

The fence is fixed at right angles to the saw cut in the baseboard. Mark the centre line for the fence, then drill and countersink the fixing holes. Prepare the fence to the dimensions given. The two holes NN for attaching an extension fence, if required, are drilled using the same technique as described above. Screw the fence on at one end and align it at right angles to the saw cut, clamp, and fix with a screw at the other end. The accuracy of this fixing determines the accuracy of your shoulder cuts, so double-check for square and make any necessary adjustments. Mark the exact position of the fence on the baseboard, then remove it while you widen the saw cut in the baseboard (using the rip fence on the tablesaw) to

SAFETY

You must provide a stop that limits the jig's travel along the table, so that it stops as soon as the blade has cleared the full width of the workpiece. A block screwed to the underside of the base will suffice.

give about $\frac{1}{16}$in (1.5mm) clearance on either side of the blade. Now screw the fence on permanently. The rail on the top of the fence is elevated by packing pieces $\frac{5}{16}$in (8mm) thick, to form a slot for the M6 bolt which secures the sliding stop. The stop locates on the top of the fence assembly and is held in place by a penny washer and wing nut on the M6 bolt.

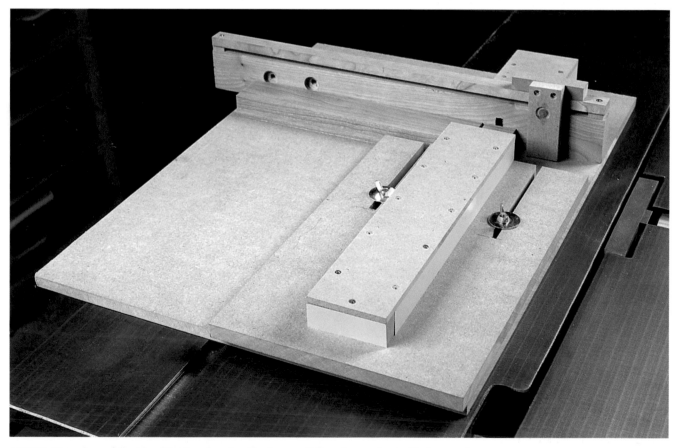

ABOVE Rear view of the shoulder jig, showing the fence, sliding stop and rear blade guard.

If an extension fence is required, it can be made to the same dimensions as the main fence, but obviously you will not need the opening for the saw blade. Clamp it in place and use the screw holes in the main fence as a guide for drilling the holes in the extension. This ensures the two mate together when the main fence is in place. The stop on the extension fence is built out $25/32$in (20mm) – the thickness of the main fence – to allow for the fact that the two fences are not flush with one another.

Blade guards and clamping piece

The construction of these parts should be sufficiently clear from the drawings.

The clamping piece is secured in place with washers and wing nuts on the M6 bolts installed in the baseboard.

Screw the runner back on the underside of the baseboard; wax the contact surfaces so the jig moves smoothly along the table.

Using the shoulder-cutting jig

Fit the jig onto the saw table, having first checked that the blade is perpendicular to the table. Set the blade height to give the depth of shoulder you require. Retract the clamping piece to allow the workpiece to fit in between it and the fence. Set the stop on the fence to the correct distance from the end of the workpiece and lock down. Now bring up the clamping piece and tighten the two bolts. You are now ready to cut the shoulders. Cut the first, then turn over the work and cut the opposite side.

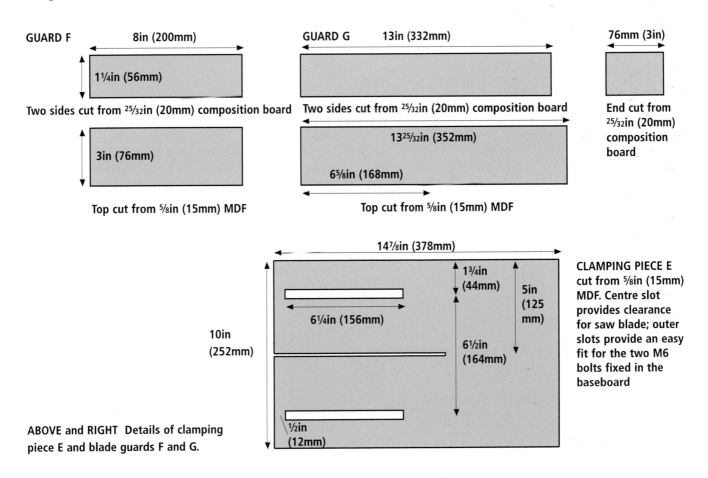

GUARD F 8in (200mm)

1¼in (56mm)

Two sides cut from $25/32$in (20mm) composition board

3in (76mm)

Top cut from ⅝in (15mm) MDF

GUARD G 13in (332mm)

Two sides cut from $25/32$in (20mm) composition board

$13^{25}/32$in (352mm)

$6^5/8$in (168mm)

Top cut from ⅝in (15mm) MDF

76mm (3in)

End cut from $25/32$in (20mm) composition board

14⅞in (378mm)

1¾in (44mm)

5in (125 mm)

6¼in (156mm)

6½in (164mm)

10in (252mm)

½in (12mm)

CLAMPING PIECE E cut from ⅝in (15mm) MDF. Centre slot provides clearance for saw blade; outer slots provide an easy fit for the two M6 bolts fixed in the baseboard

ABOVE and RIGHT Details of clamping piece E and blade guards F and G.

3:2   Tenoning jigs

Cheek-cutting jig

ABOVE The cheek-cutting jig in use, showing the workpiece clamped against the register strip on the upright fence.

This jig consists of the following parts:

- A baseboard, with a runner underneath as before.
- An L-shaped fence assembly, to which the workpiece is clamped vertically. This slides at right angles to the blade.
- A set of guards which totally enclose the saw blade: the first (B) covers the blade before entry, the second (C) as it leaves the cut. The gap between guards B and C is determined by the maximum width of stock to be cut. The portion of blade exposed between B and C is covered by guard D at the rear, and by the fence in front.
- A pair of transparent top guards, which can be adjusted to cover any gaps between the others.

RIGHT Exploded drawing of the cheek-cutting jig. The upright part of the fence has been omitted so the parts behind it can be seen.

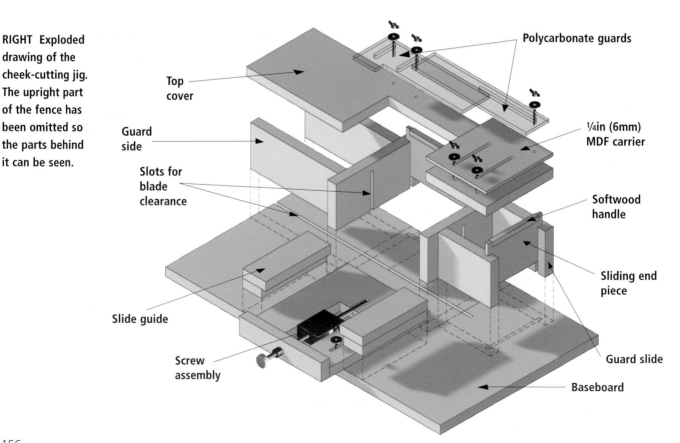

Polycarbonate guards

Top cover

Guard side

Slots for blade clearance

Slide guide

Screw assembly

¼in (6mm) MDF carrier

Softwood handle

Sliding end piece

Guard slide

Baseboard

Dimensions

The version shown allows a tenon cheek length of 1¾in (45mm) and a stock size of 6 x 2⅜in (150 x 60mm). You may want to adjust it to suit your own requirements. Determine the length of the guards as before, by raising the blade to the required height and measuring the length of exposed blade. Guard B has to cover the whole of this width, and guard C rather more than half of it. To fit stock 6in (150mm) wide, the space between B and C should be 8in (200mm). The maximum thickness of stock to be cut determines the fence travel – in this case 2½in (65mm).

Construction

Most components are made from ²⁵⁄₃₂in (20mm) composition board. This provides the required rigidity, but MDF will do as well.

Baseboard and runner

Make the baseboard to the dimensions given, and make the hardwood runner a close sliding fit in the mitre slot, as before.

The runner is a little longer than the base, so that it protrudes from the front, which makes it easier to locate the jig in the mitre slot. It fixes to the base with countersunk screws at 4in (100mm) spacing. Position the runner so the blade is 4⅝in (115mm) from the outer edge of the base; ensure that the runner is square to the leading edge of the base.

Position the base on the table and make a 12in (300mm) saw cut which will serve as a reference for setting the fence position. Mark the exact position of the runner, then remove it for the time being.

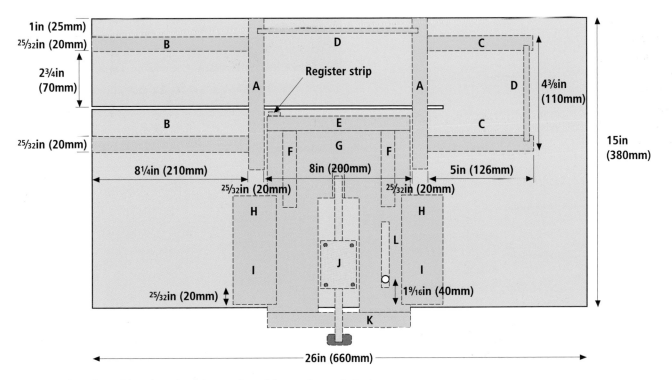

ABOVE Plan view of baseboard, with guards and fence shown dotted.

3:2   Tenoning jigs

Fence assembly

Cut out the fence components to the dimensions given. A number of them require smooth, accurate 90° edges; this can be achieved using a router table, as described for the hardwood runner on page 152.

The fence moves in and out by means of a screw which passes through the end rail of the fence and drives against a screw block fixed to the jig baseboard. Either ¼in (M6) or 5⁄16in (M8) threaded rod can be used; M6 gives finer control, M8 is more robust. There are three ways to make the screw block:

1 Drill a clearance hole through the hardwood block, let a nut into one end and fix it with epoxy. Unless the nut is level, the fence will bind; use the threaded rod to hold it in place while curing.
2 For a smoother motion, fit a second nut at the other end of the block. To ensure alignment, coat the recess for the second nut with epoxy and draw it into place with the threaded rod.
3 To make the unit still more precise, use a metal block, tapped to a depth of 1in (25mm).

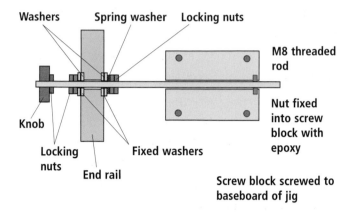

ABOVE Details of the screw assembly, with wooden screw block.

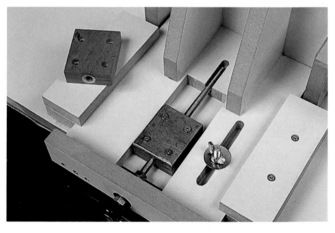

ABOVE Two alternative screw blocks, in wood and metal.

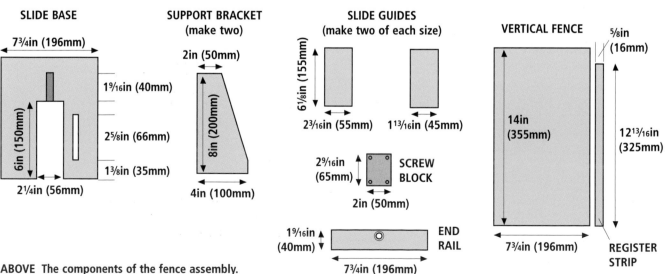

ABOVE The components of the fence assembly.

The end rail of the fence is drilled with a clearance hole for the threaded rod, then washers are let into the sides and fixed with epoxy, making sure the faces are smooth. The rod is positioned with two pairs of locking nuts, one on each side of the rail. A washer is placed between the locking nuts and the fixed washer, with a spring washer on one side to take up any backlash. The locking nuts are then adjusted so the thread can turn without any play. The knob can be made from whatever you have to hand. Assemble the slide base, vertical fence and supporting bracket, making sure they are at right angles to each other. The register strip glued to the face of the fence must be precisely perpendicular to the baseboard, so that the workpiece butted against it will be exactly vertical. The base is fixed with countersunk screws.

Blade guards

Fit the bridge pieces A and the side pieces B and C, using countersunk screws from below; leave the top cover off for now. Align the front edge of the fence with the saw cut in the base, so the fence sits centrally between the two bridge pieces. Screw the two slide guides in position from above so the fence slides back and forth without sideways play. A paper or thin plastic shim gives sufficient clearance for the fence to slide freely. Remove the fence and enlarge the saw cut in the base so the blade has slight clearance; the length of the slot must allow for the maximum cut needed to clear the workpiece. Before screwing the top cover in position, fit the bolts that will be needed to attach the carrier and the transparent top guards.

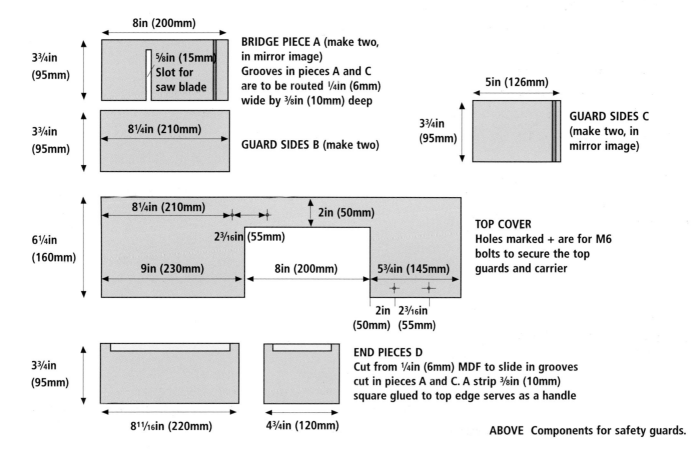

8in (200mm)

3¾in (95mm)

⅝in (15mm) Slot for saw blade

BRIDGE PIECE A (make two, in mirror image)
Grooves in pieces A and C are to be routed ¼in (6mm) wide by ⅜in (10mm) deep

3¾in (95mm)

8¼in (210mm)

GUARD SIDES B (make two)

5in (126mm)

3¾in (95mm)

GUARD SIDES C (make two, in mirror image)

6¼in (160mm)

8¼in (210mm)

2in (50mm)

2³⁄₁₆in (55mm)

9in (230mm)

8in (200mm)

5¾in (145mm)

TOP COVER
Holes marked + are for M6 bolts to secure the top guards and carrier

2in (50mm) **2³⁄₁₆in (55mm)**

3¾in (95mm)

8¹¹⁄₁₆in (220mm)

4¾in (120mm)

END PIECES D
Cut from ¼in (6mm) MDF to slide in grooves cut in pieces A and C. A strip ⅜in (10mm) square glued to top edge serves as a handle

ABOVE Components for safety guards.

3:2   Tenoning jigs

Attaching the fence

An M6 bolt must be fitted vertically into the baseboard to engage the slot L of the fence base; this will form the locking screw to fix the fence in position. The bolt is installed in the baseboard as previously described on page 153.

Put the fence back and locate the screw block to the base. The position of the screw block limits the extent of the fence travel, so make sure that this will be adequate for the work you intend to do before fixing the block in position.

Lock the fence in position by threading a washer and wing nut onto the locking screw in the base. Drill clearance holes for wood screws to fix the end rail to the fence base. Put together the screw assembly and thread it through the screw block, drawing the end rail tight to the fence base to ensure correct alignment, then fix the end rail with screws.

Top guards

The clear ¼in (6mm) polycarbonate guards do not obstruct visibility. The material can be machined with normal cutters, but will melt if allowed to get hot.

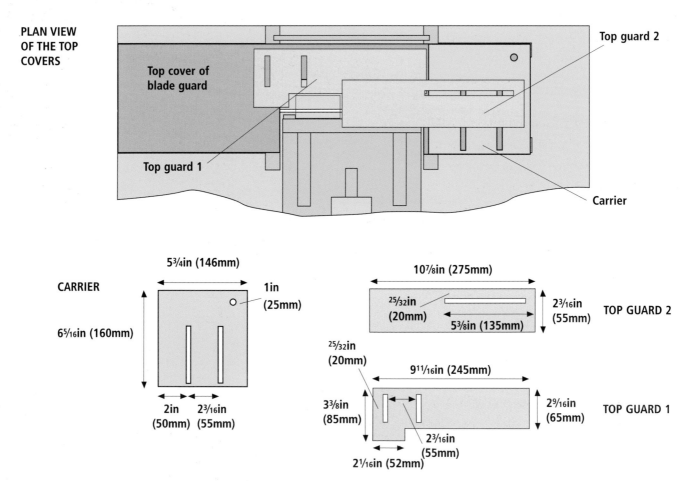

PLAN VIEW OF THE TOP COVERS

Top cover of blade guard

Top guard 1

Top guard 2

Carrier

CARRIER

5¾in (146mm)

6⁵/₁₆in (160mm)

1in (25mm)

2in (50mm)   2³/₁₆in (55mm)

10⁷/₈in (275mm)

²⁵/₃₂in (20mm)

5⅜in (135mm)

2³/₁₆in (55mm)

TOP GUARD 2

²⁵/₃₂in (20mm)

9¹¹/₁₆in (245mm)

3⅜in (85mm)

2³/₁₆in (55mm)

2⁹/₁₆in (65mm)

TOP GUARD 1

2¹/₁₆in (52mm)

ABOVE Details of the top guards and carrier.

The ¼in (6mm) MDF carrier piece and guards are secured with washers and wing nuts to the M6 bolts already installed.

Now reattach the runner to the underside of the fence; wax the contact surfaces so the jig moves smoothly along the saw table.

Using the cheek-cutting jig

Fit the jig onto the saw table, having first checked that the blade is perpendicular to the table. Screw the fence back to accommodate the workpiece, on which the shoulder cuts have already been made. Mount the workpiece on the jig against the fence register strip and clamp it to the upright part of the fence. Raise the saw blade, advance the jig and set the depth of cut required. Pull the jig back and adjust the fence to the amount that needs to be taken off the workpiece; make it slightly less than the final cut. Lock the fence and put all the guards in place – the clear polycarbonate guards can be moved around as necessary to cover any gaps – then make the cut. Turn the workpiece over and make the cut on the other side. Check how much more needs to be taken off to make the tenon fit the mortise; a limited turn on the screw is required for cut adjustment. You can now make any number of identical cuts.

If you make the shoulder cuts a little deeper than strictly necessary – about .008in (8 thou, 0.5mm), then the cheek cut does not interfere with the shoulder, and the score mark on the cheek acts as a reservoir for surplus glue when the joint is assembled.

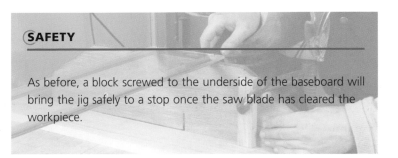

SAFETY

As before, a block screwed to the underside of the baseboard will bring the jig safely to a stop once the saw blade has cleared the workpiece.

BELOW The fully assembled jig, with a workpiece clamped in place.

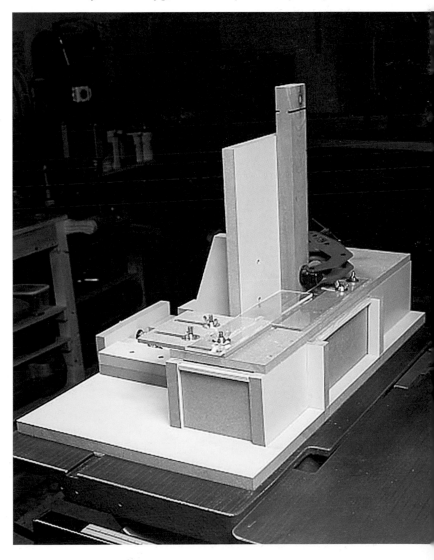

3:3   Mitre jig

Perfect mitres are a frequent requirement for woodworkers, but the mitre fence can be wearisome to set up accurately; this very simple jig will save a lot of time.

Like many good tablesaw jigs, it has two hardwood guide runners on the underside of the baseboard which fit into the mitre slots of the saw table. A hardwood rail across the leading edge of the jig provides stability and a mounting for the blade guard. The guard is cut from clear acrylic, screwed to hardwood edge supports, and is bolted to the rail, with slots to permit adjustment. The recess below the rail allows wider stock to protrude through during the cutting operation.

The two hardwood fences are glued and screwed into position, perpendicular to each other and at 45° to the blade, so that mitres can be cut to either side and will mate perfectly. Make them sturdy enough to support the work securely, whether it is hand-held or clamped to the jig.

This particular jig is restricted to 45° cuts, but this is the angle most commonly used. If your work involves cutting a wide range of angles, as in some avenues of carpentry, a sliding compound saw might be advisable.

ABOVE The paired 45° fences allow cutting to either side of the blade.

ABOVE A simple mitre-cutting jig.

3:4 Taper jig

This simple jig is ideal for cutting furniture legs and other tapered or wedge-shaped items which are commonly required.

The baseboard has a single hardwood runner which sits securely in the tablesaw's mitre slot so that the edge of the board runs flush to the saw blade. (This is easily achieved by using the tablesaw itself to cut the board to size after installing the runner.) An adjustable fence allows for the tapering of all four sides of the workpiece. The fence is mounted on a hardwood back stop to support the work as it passes through the blade. A freely rotating stop block supports the free end of the fence. For adjustment, the two bolts with wing nuts slide laterally in routed slots, which are stepped on the underside so that the bolt heads do not protrude.

Choose the dimensions to suit the work you wish to do. The example shown has a baseboard of ½in (12mm) plywood measuring 39 x 10in (1000 x 255mm), and a fence of straight-grained hardwood, 36 x 1½in (900 x 38mm).

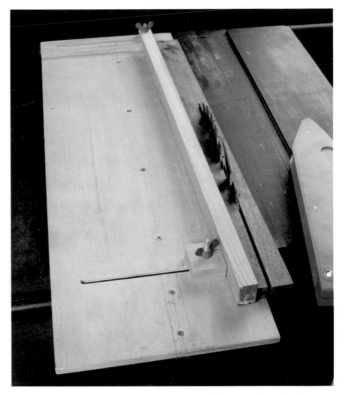

ABOVE **This basic taper jig is designed to be used with the tablesaw's own blade guard, here removed for clarity.**

ABOVE **A simple bolt and wing nut is sufficient to hold the fence securely.**

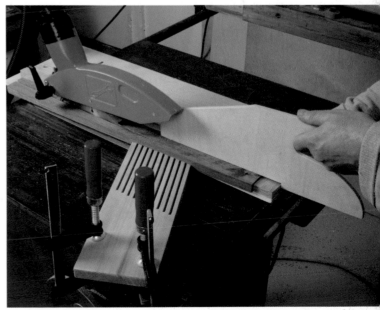

ABOVE **With the aid of a fingerboard for additional support and a slim push stick, tapered work is easily carried out.**

3:5   Bevel jig

This 45° bevel jig, resembling the traditional 'donkey's ear' shooting board, is a useful alternative to tilting the saw blade to the desired angle. Tilting the blade is an easy enough operation, but the angle will need constant checking to make sure alignment is correct, and regular tilting puts stresses upon the operating mechanism, causing the blade to move out of line with the indicating scale located at the front of the tablesaw.

I used ½in (12mm) ply, making the main box structure 24in (600mm) long, 6in (150mm) high and 6in (150mm) deep. Three 1in (25mm) pine buttresses support the face at the required 45° angle. The whole assembly is secured with countersunk screws, and glued if desired. The plywood face sits proud of the supports to which it is fixed; the substantial overhang at the top allows the work to be clamped to the jig as it passes through the blade. No runner is needed on the underside: this jig is guided by the tablesaw's rip fence.

Whether the mitre cut is on the edge or the end of the workpiece, it should marry up seamlessly with another mating board.

ABOVE A sturdy bevelling jig.

ABOVE The face of the bevelling jig is inclined at 45° to the saw table.

RIGHT The workpiece is clamped to the 45° face of the bevelling jig.

SAFETY

This jig should never be used without the blade guard and riving knife, and the workpiece should be clamped to the jig so that hands stay well away from the blade.

3:6   Slip-feather jig

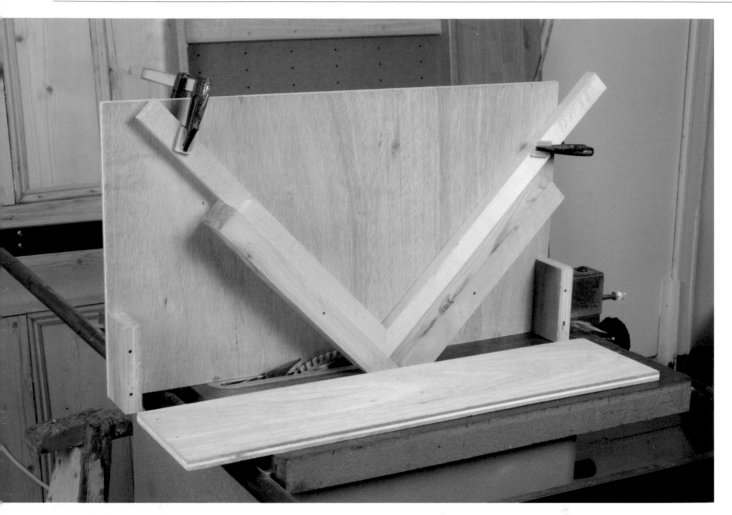

ABOVE The slip-feather jig set up for use, but with its front panel removed to show the workings.

The slip feather or spline is a useful way of giving both mechanical strength and added gluing surface to a mitre joint, along with a pleasing overall look. The apparatus required to make the slots for the feathers is essentially an upright mitre jig.

Encased within a box structure, the mitred corners of the workpieces are clamped securely to two solid hardwood supports fixed at 45° to the blade. The corner rests flush on the table top or slightly above. The blade is then set to the desired height and the workpiece is lined up, using the rip fence to guide

the jig. Then the whole assembly, butted firmly up to the rip fence, is moved forward through the saw blade, leaving a notch in the corner of the workpiece to receive the spline.

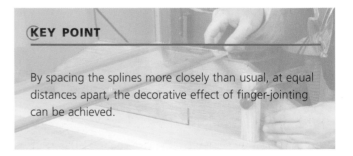

KEY POINT

By spacing the splines more closely than usual, at equal distances apart, the decorative effect of finger-jointing can be achieved.

ABOVE The supports (shown here with the front guard removed) hold the clamped workpiece at 45° to the blade.

If a single spline is to be used, it is usually placed in the centre of the wood's thickness. For work which is over 1in (25mm) thick it is advisable to use two splines, placed at one third of the thickness of the material from each edge. The thicker the material, the more splines can be added.

The jig's front covering (removed in the photographs) acts as a safety guard. This means that the blade is not really visible when making the cut, so you will need to measure the thickness of the back board and the distance from rip fence to blade. Make a cut on a test piece first, just to be sure.

The back board is ½in (12mm) ply, measuring about 24 x 18in (600 x 450mm), and the front piece is 24 x 6in (600 x 150mm). You can change these dimensions to suit the work you wish to do. The two plywood pieces screw into end supports of 1in (25mm) pine measuring 6 x 3in (150 x 75mm). The two hardwood fences, measuring 10 x 3 x 1½in (255 x 75 x 38mm), sit centrally, at exactly 45° to the blade, and are glued and screwed with countersunk screws. The corner of the resulting V is removed so that its inside corner rests on the table top, supporting the leading corner of the workpiece flush with the table top or just above it.

ABOVE A single spline through the centre of the mitre joint.

3:7 Jig for raised panels

ABOVE The raised-panel jig in use.

ABOVE A panel clamped to the inclined face of the jig. The blade guard has been removed for clarity; the jig must never be used without it.

Rather like the bevelling jig described earlier, this jig, used in conjunction with the rip fence of the tablesaw, will hold a panel upright on its near-vertical face, allowing a shallow bevel to be sawn along the edge of the workpiece. The panel is clamped in place and, with hands safely placed on top of the jig face, the work is moved through the blade, which should be raised to a height which corresponds to the width of the desired bevel. The angle of the bevel is usually between 10 and 20°.

The base, of 12mm (½in) ply, measures 24 x 3in (600 x 75mm), the back board is 24 x 6in (600 x 150mm), and the front panel is 24 x 12in (600 x 300mm). The three internal buttresses of 1in (25mm) constructional pine measure 6 x 3in (150 x 75mm), with one side cut to the desired angle to hold the jig face.

Having decided on the bevel angle required, cut the three buttresses to size. They are then glued and screwed to the back board and baseboard with countersunk screws. The face of the jig stands at double the height of the back board, and again is glued and screwed, the screws being countersunk so there is no interference with the workpiece.

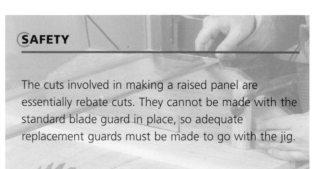

SAFETY

The cuts involved in making a raised panel are essentially rebate cuts. They cannot be made with the standard blade guard in place, so adequate replacement guards must be made to go with the jig.

ABOVE This simple home-made blade guard must be clamped to the saw table in front of the jig.

ABOVE A safety guard will have to be made for use when cutting the waste material from the face of the panel. In this case a sheet of clear acrylic has been fastened to the rip fence.

Since this jig cannot be used with a standard blade guard, a purpose-made guard is required, unless your saw has a pull-over guard system. A simple solution is a length of clear acrylic plastic running the length of the table, fixed with flat-headed screws to a sturdy piece of timber which overhangs the table just enough to allow for clamping.

Once you have made the bevel cut on all four sides of the panel, it is then laid face down on the table and the waste cut away, leaving the raised panel in the centre. Once again, proper attention needs to be paid to user safety, as this cut cannot be made with the standard blade guard in place. If a crown guard is not available, you will have to construct an adequate guard of your own. The rip fence on my tablesaw has bolt holes for a moulding-head guard, and I used these to attach a sturdy piece of acrylic which functions as a blade guard. If your saw does not have this facility, you could make something along the same lines as the guard used with the panel-raising jig, to give protection from the blade and clear visibility.

When cutting is complete, providing the blade is set to the right height and the rip fence to the correct distance from the blade, you should be left with a decoratively raised panel requiring little finishing.

BELOW The finished panel.

Resources

ALT Saws & Spares Ltd
www.altsawsandspares.co.uk

Wilhelm Altendorf GmbH & Co KG
www.altendorf.com
www.altendorfamerica.com
www.altendorf.com.au

Atkinson-Walker (Saws) Ltd
Tel. +44 (0)114 272 4748

E.Crowley & Son Ltd
www.crowleysaws.com

Delta Machinery
www.deltamachinery.com

DeWalt
www.dewalt.com
www.dewalt.co.uk

Felder Maschinenbau
www.felder.at

Festool
www.festool.co.uk
www.festoolusa.com

Health and Safety Executive (UK)
www.hse.gov.uk

Jet
www.woodmachinery.co.uk

Laguna Tools
lagunatools.com

Makita
www.makita.com

National Safety Council (USA)
www.nsc.org

NMA (Agencies) Ltd
www.nmauk.com

Powermatic
www.powermatic.com

Record Power Ltd
www.recordpower.co.uk

Rutlands Ltd
www.rutlands.co.uk

SawStop LLC
www.sawstop.com

Scheppach GmbH
www.scheppach.com

SCM/Minimax
www.woodwork.it
www.minimax-usa.com
www.scmgb.co.uk

Scott and Sargeant Woodworking Machinery Ltd
www.machines4wood.com

Sedgwick Woodworking Machinery
Tel. +44 (0)113 257 0637

Triton
www.tritontools.co.uk
www.triton-uk.com

Wadkin UltraCare Ltd
www.wadkin.com

Wealden Tool Company
www.wealdentool.com

Photo credits

Photographs are by Anthony Bailey, © GMC Publications Ltd, with the following exceptions: SawStop LLC (pp. 12 top right, 96), DeWalt (pp. 12 bottom, 14, 16, 17 top, 128 left, 129 mid, 131 top), Record Power (pp. 13 bottom, 18, 19, 42 mid, 95 top, 108, 132 top), Festool (p. 15), Stuart King (p. 22 right), Sedgwick Woodworking Machinery (pp. 26–7), E. Crowley & Son Ltd (pp. 70, 72, 76 right, 77 bottom, 81).

Glossary

Anti-kickback pawls
A safety device sometimes fitted to a riving knife, whose serrated edges help to hold the workpiece in place as it is cut.

Arbor
The metal shaft or axle which is turned by the motor and onto which the tablesaw blade is fitted.

Auxiliary fence
A shop-bought or home-made fence to replace or extend an existing one, giving more support for the work during the cutting process.

Bench-mounted saw
A variety of portable saw.

Bevel cut
A cut made with the blade tilted from the vertical.

Blade guard
An essential safety component, shop-bought or home-made to protect the operator from the moving blade.

Box joint or finger joint
A corner joint made up of interlocking 'fingers'.

Bushes
Specially made washers used to reduce the size of a hole (in a tablesaw blade, for example) to allow correct fitting of a spindle.

Cabinet saw
A heavy, floor-standing tablesaw with an enclosed base, taking blades of 10in (250mm) or over.

Chop saw
A machine in which a circular saw blade is pulled down onto the workpiece from above.

Combination blade
A blade which can be used effectively for both ripping and crosscutting.

Compound mitre
A mitre which is angled in two directions, made with the blade tilted and with the mitre fence at an angle to the blade.

Contractor's saw
Another name for the site saw.

Cradle
The framework supporting the main internal components of the tablesaw: motor, arbor, etc.

Crosscut
A cut made across the grain of the wood.

Crosscut blade
One with 40 or more teeth, giving a finer finish than a ripping blade.

Dado, housing, grooving, trenching
Different terms for a channel cut with or across the grain.

Dado head
A blade or set of blades mounted on a hub to make wide cuts (dados) in a workpiece; its use is now discouraged on safety grounds.

Dial indicator
A precision instrument used to measure runout.

Dimensioning
The process of cutting a workpiece to the required measurements.

European saw
A US term for a standard European cabinet saw with sliding table.

Feed speed
The rate at which the work is moved through the saw blade.

Fence
An adjustable guide used to control the workpiece and help steer it through the saw blade.

Glossary

Fingerboard or featherboard
A safety accessory used to hold the workpiece firmly against the rip fence or table top during cutting.

Flip-over saw
A dual-action machine which can be used as an ordinary circular saw or as a mitre-cutting machine.

Hold-down
A safety accessory, bought or improvised, providing downward pressure to hold a workpiece in place as it passes through the saw.

Infeed table
An extension table providing additional support on the front (operator's side) of the main table.

Isolator switch
A safety device, mounted on the machine or on the wall, to cut off electrical current in an emergency or when the machine is to be left unattended.

Jig
Any kind of accessory, often home-made, which serves to make a repetitive precision job easier and more efficient.

Kerf
The cut made by a saw blade.

Kickback
The dangerous situation in which a moving saw blade forcibly ejects the workpiece back towards the operator.

Microfilter
A device for extracting the dangerous, minute dust particles created during cutting.

Microgauge
A measuring device which indicates the amount of incremental cut desired.

Mitre cut
An angled cut made across the face, edge or end of a workpiece.

Mitre gauge
An adjustable guide used to steer and control the workpiece as it is crosscut.

Mitre saw
Similar to a chop saw, but can also be turned to the side to cut various angles, including compound mitres.

Mitre slot
A channel milled into the table top parallel with the blade, in which the mitre gauge slides freely along the saw table.

Moulding head
A cutting device, fitted to the arbor in place of the ordinary blade, in which sets of cutting blocks shape the workpiece; now discouraged on safety grounds.

Movement (in timber)
Any change in the shape or size of the wood caused by water absorption or loss, or by the release of internal stresses when the wood is cut.

Non-through cut
A cut in which the blade does not pass right through the wood.

Outboard support
Any device providing additional support to the workpiece at the rear or side of the main table.

Pitch
A resinous residue on a saw blade, which creates friction and heat during cutting.

Portable saw
A smaller type of tablesaw, with a blade diameter not exceeding 10in (250mm).

Pull saw
A form of site saw in which the blade is pulled through the workpiece by means of a handle.

Push stick
An essential safety accessory used to help guide a workpiece through the saw without the operator's hands coming near the blade.

Rebate (or rabbet)
An L-shaped channel cut along the edge of a workpiece.

Resawing
A technique in which thick stock is sawn down into thinner boards.

Rip cut
A cut made along the grain.

Ripping blade
A blade designed to cut with the grain, with deep gullets and substantial hook angles.

Riving knife
A scythe-like device fitted just behind the blade to prevent the cut timber from pinching the blade, causing kickback.

Runout
The amount by which a rotating component runs out of true.

Scoring blade
A small saw blade performing an initial cut prior to the main cut, giving a finer finish.

Sheet material
Timber or man-made board sold in a standard size of 8 x 4ft (2440 x 1220mm).

Shim
A washer or other spacer inserted to correct a slight misalignment between components.

Site saw
A machine with the same blade size as a portable saw, but of sturdier build.

Sled
A home-made carriage which runs squarely on the table top to convey the wood safely through the saw blade for ripping or crosscutting.

Sliding table or carriage
An additional table which runs alongside the main table, helping to guide the wood for accurate cutting.

Splitter
US term for a riving knife.

Switch cover
A home-made safety device which allows the off-switch to be operated with the knee when the user's hands are otherwise occupied.

Tablesaw
A generic term covering various types of machine with table-mounted circular saw blades. In this book, the term normally refers to the cabinet saw unless otherwise stated.

TCT
Tungsten-carbide-tipped (referring to teeth on a saw blade).

Tear-out
An unsightly ragged edge, typically caused by an unsupported saw cut.

Throat plate or table insert
A component surrounding the saw blade, covering the opening which gives access to the arbor.

Trunnions
Semicircular brackets holding the cradle and allowing for pivotal movement.

Universal or combination machine
A large-scale, multipurpose woodworking machine.

Zero-tolerance throat plate
A throat plate or table insert which leaves almost no clearance between itself and the saw blade.

Index